D0629123

Continuing Education

BOOKS BY DOROTHY WEIL

In Defense of Women: Susanna Rowson (1762–1824)

134334

Continuing Education

Dorothy Weil

813.54
W 422c

Rawson, Wade Publishers, Inc. / New York

Alverno College
Library Media Center
Milwaukee, Wisconsin

Library of Congress Cataloging in Publication Data
Weil, Dorothy.
   Continuing education.
   I. Title.
PZ4.W4214Co   [PS3573.E3837]   813'.5'4   78-72895
ISBN 0-89256-096-7

Copyright © 1979 by Dorothy Weil
All rights reserved.
Published simultaneously in Canada by McClelland and
Stewart, Ltd.
Manufactured in the United States of America
by
Designed by E. O'Connor
First Edition

To Sidney with love

Continuing Education

Chapter 1

I was the only woman on my street who had never had a Cuisinart or a hysterectomy. Or even an affair. I felt there was something wrong with me. When I mentioned my anxiety to my friends and family, they all agreed that there was.

Several winked knowingly: "You're thirty-eight—and neither you nor Bert has ever—c'mon, you're kidding." Our doctor advocated hysterectomies as a routine procedure; that "damned thing" would be causing me trouble soon. But I had gone to see him for poison ivy, and I decided major surgery wasn't called for. My friend Judy said, "Why don't you just get a Cuisinart? You'll love it."

"No I won't," I said. "I've just had the kitchen redone. For the first time in my life it's completely clean and I'm thinking of having it sealed off."

"Then you'd better get a college degree."

That was the other thing I didn't have that most of my friends were "into."

I thought of all those paintings and drawings stacked in the basement; the ones I'd done while the children were small. I'd never taken them to a dealer or even entered them in a show, but had always vaguely thought of them as leading to a career—someday in the future.

"I just threw all my old magazines and clippings away

last week," I said to Judy. "I realized I'm not going to be a Broadway set designer or a famous fashion illustrator."

"Maybe not, but you can do *something*. You paint beautifully, but this is a credential society; you need a degree. You could teach . . ."

"Yuck."

"You're a prime candidate for empty-nest syndrome," she warned. "Gail is in college. Barney will be leaving before you know it—two years?"

"Donald's only nine," I said.

"Donald does not need a mother," Judy replied. "Donald needs a small country to run."

"But what would happen to my home? Every time I go shopping, something happens. The last time, the cat got into the varnish and was stuck to the couch when I got home."

"Excuses, excuses," said Judy. "Millions of women are going back to school. You just can't face the challenge."

"It's Bert I can't face," I replied.

"Well, Bert has to join the twentieth century. Most men don't come home for lunch—*really* they don't, Laura."

I was beginning to weaken. Judy was not the first to pick on me this way. My collegiate daughter Gail had also given me a going-over about my unraised consciousness, my moldering talent, my wasted life.

"I raised you three children," I said in my defense. Gail looked at me as though I wore double-knits.

"That's hardly a life's work," she scoffed, "and when we're gone—then what?"

"I haven't been in a studio, or written a paper for eighteen years!" I said to Judy. "Why don't *you* go back to school?"

She winked leeringly.

"I," said Judy, "have a Cuisinart."

I was convinced. I had been thinking about doing the very thing Judy mentioned, just before she brought it up. I called the art department at City University and asked the secretary to send me a catalogue. Soon a thick red pamphlet arrived in the mail, and with my hands clammy and shaking, I read of the delights that might be mine:

BASIC DRAWING 203; 3 cr. hrs. M.W.F.; 10:00–11:00; Req.
GRAPHICS 101; 4 cr. hrs. Tu.Thurs.; 1:00–2:30; Opt.

The introduction to the catalogue assured me that these uninspiring items would provide me with a broad, well-rounded program in the basic arts, prepare me to make acceptable vocational choices, and help me to be a better citizen in a democratic society.

Surely my family could not object to so worthy a set of goals. But, I thought in panic: would the art department make me repeat Basic Drawing? I'd taken that in my three years at the Academy. Would I have to take the scholastic requirements—like Freshman English? I could just see the Disney Studios making a movie of my new life. It would be like a rerun of an old Fred MacMurray picture: *Mother Was a Freshman* or something.

I decided I'd better wait until the summer quarter to register. Beginning in spring quarter, though apparently permissible, would cause problems. Some of the courses were continuations of fall and winter classes. Waiting would give me time to prepare my family. And myself.

"Would you have to take math?" asked Donald.
"Probably," I said.

"Forget it."

"Maybe they'd let me out of it." I turned the pages of the catalogue. "I think there are some options. Here's something called Creative Math."

"That's a goon course," he said. "Like Inner City Life. But I'd go for it if I were you."

"But what about the whole idea?" I said. "Just think— if I were going to school, the next time you had to stay home with a cold, like today, I wouldn't be here to bring you lunch or bake cookies."

"Let's face it, Mom," said Donald, "you're a gas as a painter, but you're just not Susie Homemaker. Look how lopsided these things are!"

He held one of my home-baked cookies up for inspection. It looked like an amoeba. He bit into it. Total silence.

"These are called Peanut *Crunch*," he said.

"It's the thought that counts," I said.

"Not with cookies," said Donald. "Honest, Mom, I could take care of myself. If there's anything to stop you from going to college it's Dad."

"Oh, yes—Dad."

"He'll be home any minute. Have you got his baloney on white with mayonnaise ready?"

"Judy says men don't come home for lunch any more."

"Boy, have you got a way to go!"

I got up from my chair next to Donald's bed.

"Are you sure you'd be all right?"

"Sure. As for Barney—I dunno—" He moved one hand in a "comme ci-comme ça" gesture. "He's getting to be kind of a punk."

"Why do you say that?"

"Well, for starters the Dracula cape and the sixties hair —not to mention the dirty tee-shirt."

Oh, thought I, the one that says "Disco Sucks."

"He'll get over all that," I said.

I wished I were sure.

"How's Donald?" asked Bert. He sat down in his chair, checked over the sandwich on his plate, and beamed at seeing everything in its place, including me. He took a bite of baloney on white.

"How was your morning?" he asked—he always does.

"So how should it be?" I said. "I ran the dishwasher, answered the phone, dusted the living room, baked Donald some cookies, read him a story to keep him from watching daytime television, and fixed his and your lunch."

"You sound a little edgy. You needn't make Donald *quite* so comfortable. I have a slight hunch he's malingering anyway."

"Why do you say that?"

"That's my line," said Bert. "I'm the psychiatrist."

He took another obviously satisfying bite of his sandwich.

"Nevertheless," I insisted, "why do you say Donald's malingering?"

"His report card was something less than satisfactory this term—and we know he can do better."

"Everyone gets colds."

"Of course. But as you know, we do tend to hurt or disable ourselves through illness or accident when there is something we don't care to face."

"If that's true I think I'm about to get pneumonia."

"How come?"

"I'm thinking about going back to school—to the art department—to get a degree."

"Why would you want to do that?"

"So I can teach—"

"Do you want to teach?"

"No."

7

"Then why? You can paint here. We can fix up the basement into a better studio. I'm all for women having some outside interest, you know that."

"Then why do you come home for lunch?"

Bert looked as though I'd put catsup on his baloney sandwich.

"I like to come home for lunch. I've always come home for lunch. I can relax away from the patients and the hospital."

"I can leave you a sandwich in the fridge after I start to school."

"I like to have you sitting right there while I sit right here and eat my baloney sandwich."

Can you believe that Bert was considered something of a pioneer in his profession?

He didn't say another word about my plans. It was as though his logic was so inexorable that I could not possibly have anything more to say on the subject.

When he came for dinner, I broached the idea again.

"Bert, I really want to go back to school. My 'outside interest,' as you put it, is not outside; it's in the basement. I have only the water bugs to talk to. It's not enough. It's just an accomplishment—like embroidery in the eighteenth century."

"But the children need you," he said. "I've seen so many children ignored by mothers out working or looking for careers. The children always get into trouble—to show they need their mothers at home. Some actually maim themselves."

We dropped the subject temporarily. Bert put on his jacket to take out the garbage. While he was carting the cans to the curb, he stepped into the storm sewer and sprained his ankle.

Chapter 2

I let the deadline for summer registration go by too. It wasn't just Bert's ankle; it was my clammy, shaking hands whenever I thought of facing a classroom.

"Wise decision," said Bert. "If you were in school we couldn't go to the cottage."

"It wasn't a decision—it was fear," I said. "And if I'd thought about the cottage, I would've signed up."

He ignored my statement. He could not believe anyone could not love the Quonset hut his mother had given him on Lake Michigan. Mosquitoes, mildew, outside johns— that was Bert's idea of heaven.

"I know every rock, every tree, every grain of sand on that beach," I said. "I hope I never see the place again."

"Oh, Laura, you don't mean that," said Bert. "Think of the fun we've had there."

I thought: all I could recall were mounds of sticky dishes and no dishwasher, tracking through morning mist to use the "biffy"—I hate that word—kids with sunburn and mosquito bites, sweat. I applied citronella, poison ivy poultices, Mexicana, while Bert chopped wood, swam, water-skied, sailed.

"Couldn't we go someplace this year?" I said. "Europe —or Mexico? Canada?"

Bert looked crushed. He was old Cincinnati. He'd spent his idyllic boyhood at the lake. He always went to the lake. Therefore, said his Cincinnati logic, he should always go to the lake.

"We'll never see the world," I complained.

"Oh, there's nothing much to see," said he. "We took the grand tour when we were sixteen—went through every cathedral and art museum in Europe. Our grandmother insisted. There's not a fresco in Europe I haven't had to memorize the painter of . . ."

"Sounds great to me."

"We can't afford Europe. I know you want more time to paint," Bert said, "so let's do this: Barney can get a summer job and Donald can go to camp so you'll have more free time. We'll take just two weeks at the cottage in July."

I counted the weeks till Labor Day.

Somehow, in spite of all the arrangements planned in my behalf, I got very little painting done. The roof had sprung a leak over the winter and it was my job to gather estimates. The roof man said the gutters were rotten and those needed work. Then a down-spout man had to be summoned and a painter called to look at inside walls that the roof leak had ruined.

Barney and Donald seemed a little reluctant about the plans we made for them.

"Why don't you just send me to prison?" asked Donald when I approached him with brochures from Camp Jolly.

"Prison?" I said. "Camp Jolly has horseback riding, canoeing, hiking, baseball, camp circle, crafts."

"So do prisons."

"What does he object to?" I asked Barney. "This camp costs eight hundred dollars and it's all geared to his age group."

"The counselors are probably fascists," said Barney. "They always are: rise and shine—lights out—sing-along time."

"But you loved camp," I said. "Remember?"

"Do I remember? I never saw a summer at home till I got my driver's license."

"You loved camp."

"Yeah—but did you have to send me two weeks before it opened?"

"Well, how would *you* like to spend your whole summer with a twelve-year-old boy?" I asked.

"I was two and a half when I started," said Barney, "and this big fruit on the bus used to beat me up every day."

"You never told me that," I said.

"I must have told Donald," he said.

Our plan that Barney should get a job met with equal enthusiasm.

"I have to practice with the band!" he exclaimed. "We're changing our whole style."

"Thank God for that," muttered Bert.

"You just changed your style," said I. "Wasn't that what the new equipment was all about?"

"That was rinky-dink stuff. We're going into punk rock. You can't get dates to play otherwise."

"But we just paid two hundred and fifty dollars for the amplifier—and you owe us—remember? You agreed to pay it off if we loaned you the money."

"We thought we'd get more offers for band dates," said Barney.

"Nevertheless, you owe the money, Barney, and you'll have to get a job—" said Bert.

Barney looked apologetic.

"Gee, Dad," he said, "I'd like to—but work really isn't my bag."

Bert handed him the want ads. Barney let them lie on the table.

"Friend of mine had a job in a pizza parlor—almost got killed," Barney said. "Guy came in with a gun and held up the place—shot the manager—would've got my friend but the bullet lodged in the dead guy's head—"

"I think we can find something less hazardous than pizza work," said Bert. "The hospital can always use an extra hand or two."

"Hospitals," said Barney. "You know I can't stand the sight of blood—"

"We'll try not to start you performing surgery right away," said Bert. "Can you stand the sight of a bedpan?"

Barney pulled his black cape around him and slunk out of the room like his hero confronted by a cross.

Barney got a job at an alcoholic drying-out clinic, but Donald escaped camp.

"Won't do to force him," said Bert.

I grabbed for my art school catalogue. But it was too late.

The summer was the usual blur of sticky glasses and knives, pop and beer cans all over the kitchen, heavy sound equipment moved in and out of the house. One day an electric piano being hauled to Barney's room took the paint off all the doors; another day a synthesizer broke a spoke out of the stair railing. Donald's collection of worms got out of their can. We went to our leaky Quonset hut in July.

Still, as Labor Day approached, I hadn't signed up for school. I showed all the signs of letting another deadline get away, when Judy stopped in to remind me of my susceptibility to mid-life crisis.

"But, Judy," I said, "the chances of a woman doing anything but mixing paints in some man's studio or being a grade school art teacher are so remote!"

"I guess you're right," she agreed. "You're better off hiding your stuff in the basement."

"Remember all the brilliant girls in our class?" I said. "We were always the top students. The senior class president was Ethel Schmerz. What good did it do her?"

"Are you talking about Dr. Schmerz?" said Judy. "She's running the psychiatric ward at the Menninger Clinic."

"Oh."

"She's still beautiful as ever, too," said Judy. "Didn't Bert date her once or twice?"

What genuine ambition won't accomplish, blind jealousy often will. The next day I called City University and talked to the dean of the art school. I was determined to get out of my rut.

Doctor Schmerz?

Chapter 3

Gloria Steinem has decreed that no woman should take more than fifteen minutes to dress, but maybe she doesn't have problem hair, dry skin, receding gums, and a fungus.

It took me a whole morning to get ready to go to the University and register. How would I ever get to classes on time? Not only were there morning dishes, two children to be gotten to school, pets to feed, and a baloney sandwich to fix, but myself put into shape to leave the house.

My bathroom looked like a torture chamber: the blow dryer and curling iron gleamed on the counter like implements used to get state secrets. The eyelash curler looked pretty horrible, too, if you didn't know what it was for; there were tweezers, scissors, sharp nail files, razors, a water pic.

I was after the natural look.

Actually, I used little makeup. I never touched eyeliner. It was just the little cranking-up, maintenance work that took longer every year. For a reasonably decent-looking, healthy person, I had an enormous collection of products and a staggering series of procedures that kept me from falling into decay—and from getting anywhere in a hurry: cleansing with a special soap for the fungus (caused by gardening), a good rub with the buff-puff in the shower, shampoo and blow-dry for the hair. Neck salve for a rash, moisturizer for the face, a touch of perfume and deodorant, a dab of hand cream. Sight-saver for my glasses, spray for the finished hair.

It was getting near my period so I downed a Librium, an Esidrix, and an iron pill for anemia.

I didn't have time to do all the things recommended to keep myself in shape *and* return to school. That was clear.

I could skip the dental floss, but then what would Virginia, the dental hygienist, say? I could just hear her lecturing about the plaque that was building up on my teeth, if I didn't do an extra-special brushing, and the softening gums that only floss could save.

Never mind the rough, unshaped fingernails, I told myself. Let's stick to the essentials.

I pulled on my panty hose, lying back on the bed with my legs in the air to get them to come up to the crotch. I tore a hole in the right leg with a jagged thumbnail.

I had put on my new fall knit, and of course the temperature was 95 degrees in Cincinnati's usual September Indian summer. It wasn't just fear that was ruining the blouse under the arms. I was dripping from every pore; my moisturizer felt slippery.

But oh to be on campus now that fall is here! I had a sense of purpose. Soon I'd be in a comfortable routine, carrying my books across campus, learning something exciting, meeting congenial souls. If only I could find a parking space.

The dirty little secret of the modern university: having to park six miles from the buildings your classes are in. Oh well, next time I'd wear flats. I was overdressed anyway in my chic little knit and high-heeled shoes. I had wanted to put my best foot forward with whomever I met on my first day, but instead I felt conspicuous among the sea of cut-off jeans, ragged tee-shirts, and hairy legs. Where were all the millions of middle-aged women returning to college? I stuffed my designer scarf inside my purse.

The lines to register for classes were very long and I was sent from one building to another like a pawn on a board game, or a ping-pong ball.

My first stop was to see an advisor who made out a schedule for me.

"Wait," I said, "you signed me up for gym. Can you picture me in a gym suit playing hockey?"

She looked up at me for the first time.

"Requirement," she said. She opened the catalogue: "Every candidate for a degree must take at least one quarter of physical education."

"I'm thirty-eight years old!" I hissed, hoping not to be heard. Every eye in the room turned toward me.

"You'll have to see the dean if you want to be excused. Do you have some physical impairment?"

"Yes," I said.

"Dean's office is in the Chemistry Building, but they're closed for lunch."

I checked the rest of the schedule. All okay. As per my agreement with Dean Pointer, I was to be a senior; he'd given me three full years' credit for the time I'd done at the Art Academy—on probation.

"Since you're older and have some life experience, we'll just throw you in and see how you do," he said. "If you can't hack it, you may have to go back to more basic courses."

"Freshman English?" I said.

"Freshman English."

The lady at the desk signed my schedule and sent me to the Physics Building to pick up registration forms. Sweating in my knit dress in an airtight room, I tried to recall my mother's birthdate, my childhood diseases.

Did I have a Social Security number? I invented one. I checked the box for married, listed my children's names, but was stumped on guardian.

"That's your husband," said the lady.

Was I his ward?

And what difference did my father's occupation make to the art department?

By the time I got to race and religion, I was getting so annoyed by silly questions I left the blanks blank. W and B didn't tell much about a person's ethnic background, and Protestant, Catholic, or Jewish seemed limited, too.

I took the packet to the next stop on the line and handed it to a man who was checking them. He glanced at my efforts, looked up at me, and checked W for race.

"What is your religion, Mrs. Hoffman?" he said. "Are you Protestant, Catholic, or Jewish?"

I was getting into the mood for a fight and I said loudly, "I am an agnostic."

"Oh," said he, without turning a hair. "Well—are you a Protestant agnostic, a Catholic agnostic, or a Jewish agnostic?"

"Just put Unitarian," I said.

I was allowed to move one space: go to the Student Union and pick up class cards. There were huge lines in front of a roomful of tables and signs indicating subjects: English, Art, Sociology, etc. The first class on my schedule, Advanced Drawing, was closed; Sculpture 202, closed. My final subject was Independent Study, which involved no classes, but was simply the name for a project done on one's own initiative.

"Independent Study is closed," said the clerk.

I started to argue but could see it would do no good. I was up against Catch 22–203.

Wondering how poor Bert was getting along eating his baloney sandwich all alone at the kitchen table, and wishing I were there with him instead of in a sweltering, none-too-clean office in the Art Building, I asked for a new schedule.

"We've added sections in all those subjects," said the advisor. She tore up my original schedule, rewrote it with new section numbers, and sent me back to the lines for class cards.

"Closed for Lunch."

I ventured down to the cafeteria myself, ate a sandwich, and drank a glass of iced tea, then retreated to the ladies' room where in a hot toilet stall I took off my panty hose, girdle, and half-slip. I looked a little lumpy but was cooler with the hose and the underwear stuffed in my purse. When I went back to the class-card lines, they had re-formed, and I inched toward the head of the line, trying to think about the larger aesthetic problems I would soon be dealing with—once I had left all this red tape behind. I still didn't see anyone who looked as old as I.

Class cards in hand, I was sent to the bursar. When I reached the window, finally, to pay my fees, the cashier looked at my packet and said, "Didn't they give you a red card?"

"No," I said desperately, "no—they said nothing about a red card. No—no one. No red card."

Her eyes turned toward me like those on a dead cod-fish. She turned to her co-worker.

"She doesn't have a red card."

"No red card?" asked the other.

I clutched the bars of the cashier's cage like a prisoner in a James Cagney movie. "Don't send me back to the lines," I wanted to shout, "please don't send me back! They said nothing—no—nothing about a red card."

The two women went into the back office—presumably

to confer about the anomaly of my missing, my derelict, my mysterious red card. I waited, with sweat pouring down my bare legs and into my shoes. I hoped I wasn't making a puddle on the floor.

After an agonizing wait that seemed like an hour, the cashier returned, stamped my packet and, with no explanation or change of expression, said, "Six hundred and twenty-nine dollars and twenty-six cents. Cash or check only, please. If paying by check, please make it out to the City University, Main Campus."

I was so grateful for my apparent release from the red card peril that I pulled my purse open, not only able but willing and eager to pay the demanded fee. I grabbed for my checkbook, caught my scarf on my wristwatch, and pulled it halfway out of my purse, throwing my panty hose and girdle toward the floor.

"I'm *terribly* sorry," I said. I leaned over swiftly to retrieve the panty hose from the sandaled foot of the boy behind me and my girdle from his briefcase—and scattered the contents of my purse all over the floor. A plastic Tampax holder rolled over into one corner and lodged beneath a soft-drink machine.

I was holding up the line; twenty-five disgruntled-looking people fidgeted as I wrote out my check and went about among them picking up hair clips, change, bottles of "Moon Drops," and Tampax.

Going back to school, Judy had distinctly said, would be good for my self-esteem.

☗ Chapter 4

"You were clearly feeling a bit of guilt and anxiety at returning to school," said Bert, when I told him about the purse.

"Guilt?" I said. "A bit of guilt? I'm eaten up with guilt! Do you think a non-guilty woman would come home from a grueling experience like that and clean the entire house, including the windows, make a soufflé for dinner, and start scrubbing the cracks in the bathroom tile with a toothbrush?"

I was always surprised that people paid fifty dollars an hour for Bert's insights. They were the sort of thing Donald came up with without trying.

"You feel ambivalent," he continued, "afraid the family and home will suffer while you're off enjoying yourself."

"And yet when I'm here," I said, "I feel so frustrated and cut off. Barney and Donald won't need me forever, you know. How did *you* do?"

"I don't like bread that's been in the refrigerator," he said.

We got through the weekend without the House of Hoffman collapsing. I was a registered, bona-fide student at the college of art. Yet the washing got done, we ate three meals a day on Saturday and Sunday, we went to the symphony Saturday night, and Barney and Donald were driven to their music lessons. Of course, classes hadn't started yet.

But I thought of nothing else. On Saturday, I bought a denim skirt; my little wool numbers were not going to do for on-campus wear. I bought some sensible shoes. God, I realized, looking through my closet—I was like a Chinese woman with bound feet—none of my shoes had less than three-inch heels or platforms—except the mules I wore around the house. And they were too old-ladyish.

"What are you looking so cat-ate-the-canary about?" said Bert on the way to the Saturday night concert.

"When people ask me what I'm doing now, I have something to say."

"But I'm really worried," said Bert.

"Oh, don't worry, I think I can handle the courses. I feel peppier getting out of the house."

"I'm not worried about you," he said. "It's me. I don't think I'm ready for this."

"You'll get used to it—things will work out."

"That's what Hoover said—and Johnson—and Chamberlain."

"It's not World War Two."

"What's on the program tonight?" he asked. "I hope it's not any of that modern stuff."

I took the program out of my purse.

"Quartet for violin and synthesizer, by Damon Wilson."

"Oh, God," Bert groaned, "another excruciating evening. Why can't they play Mozart?"

"They did last week. Maybe you'll like this."

"No, I won't," said Bert, "I've already heard everything I'm ever going to like."

"It'll be a change."

"I hate change," said Bert.

⚜ Chapter 5

My first day of class, I skipped all my beauty and maintenance routines, pulled my hair back in a ponytail, and
put on a tee-shirt and my new skirt. I arrived at school
an hour early, so I decided to look around. The smell
of paint and turpentine took me back to my earlier days
as a student at the Academy. The halls were the same
old mess: lockers stacked with canvasses and portfolios,
sinks streaked with color. Lost in nostalgia, I wandered
into a studio where I tripped over a large white wooden
beam lying on the floor.

"Ouch," I said, and bent down to hold my sneakered
toe.

"Oh, pardon me," I said to the thing. It was somebody's sculpture, "Rhyme Without Reason." How things
had changed. Our sculpture studio had been filled with
metal forms on blocks to build clay figures. This one was
filled with cardboard boxes in various sizes, called "Form,"
and welding equipment—not to mention a set of rubber
tires painted pink. I was afraid to touch the metal pillar
that looked as though it was part of the building—it might
be somebody's work and they wouldn't want my fingerprints on it. Soft sculpture in the form of birds, old ladies,
palm trees, and Volkswagens lurched all over the place.

The painting studio came as an equal shock: dominating it was a swirl of burlap that looked like a whole warehouse of gunny sacks going crazy. On the wall was a large shaggy thing—black wool, brown wool, and uncombed gray wool cascading down the white plaster in a formless mass. On a pedestal sat a small crocheted box, the yarn of which was interwoven with a few chicken feathers, some thread, and hair.

"Ghastly, isn't it?"

I turned around to see a nice-looking young man in blue jeans.

"It looks as though it were swept out from under the bed," said I, "all that hair and guck."

"House moss," he said. "That's what my grandmother called it."

He studied the burlap.

"I'm not sure I'm going to fit in," he said.

"Me neither."

"Is this your first year here?" he asked.

"I'm a senior."

"So am I—I just transferred from Pittsburgh."

The bell rang and we both laughed.

"Time for class."

It turned out that this nice young man and I were in the same morning classes. The professors did little but call the roll and give out lists of supplies and books, so my mind was not totally on class work. I found myself staring at my new acquaintance. He smiled back. I was comparing him to Barney. He was so relaxed in talking to me—he had not treated me like an "older woman," and while he was casually dressed, like all the young people, he wasn't messy. I wished Barney could be more like him. Between drawing and painting class, he asked my name.

"I'm Bob Harper," he said.

*　　*　　*

In the crush at lunch, I managed to get my tray to a table already occupied by several boys and girls, and wedged myself into a seat against the wall. Although it was only the first day of class, everyone seemed to know everyone else. The others at the table talked across me. I was relieved when my new friend Bob plopped his tray down and said, "Hi, Laura—what did you think of our profs?"

My lunch suddenly tasted good. As we wolfed down Coke and sandwiches, Bob and I chatted about what both teachers had said in their introductory remarks.

"I think I'm going to like Newman," said Bob.

"Me too. Sanders seems a little—"

"Obscure?"

"Exactly."

"Where do you go from here?"

"Sculpture."

"I'm taking Graphics," he said. "So this is good-bye— at least for now. Maybe we could have a beer later at Wolfie's."

"Oh, I've gotta go home and fix dinner for my kids," I blurted out.

"You've got *kids?*" he said. His surprise seemed genuine.

"Three—a nine-year-old and a sixteen-year-old—"

"*You've* got a teenager?" he cried.

I didn't tell him about the one in college.

Bob covered his face with his hands.

"I was asking you for a date," he said. "And I was dreaming of the day we might even move in together."

"Oh."

We both burst out laughing.

"Do I owe you an apology?" he asked.

"No—I owe you my eternal thanks—"

He studied me again, closely.

"You're not divorced, are you?"

"Happily married."

"Well, be careful; there are lots of unscrupulous males around here. And here's my card in case you decide to dump your old man."

As we finished lunch, I thought: When he's thirty, I'd be forty-four; when he's forty, I'd be fifty-four. It didn't sound half bad.

After lunch I rushed to the ladies' room. I felt twenty-five years younger than I had when I registered. I looked younger too—with the ponytail and no makeup.

"How was your first day at school?" asked Bert at dinner.

"It was great—just great!" I said.

"You look full of beans. What happened?"

"Some guy about twenty-four years old made a pass at me."

"I don't blame him," said Bert. "You look like a teen-ager in that get-up. But how were the classes?"

"They were okay too."

Later, in bed, Bert asked me about the pass.

"What did the kid do? I mean—"

"Oh—nothing serious. Just asked me out for a beer—and if I'd like to move in with him."

"You weren't tempted, were you?"

I laughed loudly.

"Oh, don't be silly! I've got three children!"

"And a husband," said Bert.

"And a husband."

That night I dreamed that a young man seven feet tall named Zero Cholesterol came zooming up to the house and drove me away in a soft, pink velvet Volkswagen.

Chapter 6

My euphoria did not last. The washing began to pile up, the meals became less appetizing and more erratic. Every assignment at school seemed to clash with some assignment at home. I could please neither Bert nor Mr. Borges, my art history professor.

Our class met the second day of school, and Mr. Borges and I got off on the wrong foot right away. Shuffling through our class cards, he called "Sarah," "Steve," "George," etc., until he came to me; then he got formal.

"Mrs. Bertrand Huffman?" he said.

"Hoffman," said I, "Laura Hoffman."

"*Mrs.* Hoffman." He took a long, disapproving look at me. The high I felt over Bob Harper's mistaking me for a young woman disappeared. I looked around for another matron in the room, but my fellow students seemed to have gotten even younger.

"You're not a nurse, are you?"

He seemed to be searching for reasons why a decrepit character like me would be in a first-year course.

"Art major," I said.

"Oh, a grade school teacher."

"No, an art major. I'm a painter."

"A nice hobby, art. Something to do between yoga class and Great Books."

With me as an implicit example of dilettantism, Borges launched into a long tirade on the seriousness of creative endeavor, the glory of the Middle Ages, "before the arts became effeminate," and the paucity of good art today.

Actually, when he got going, he was quite interesting. I even agreed with him on some points. But I certainly didn't like him.

At the end of the first class period, Professor Borges gave us purple-inked ditto sheets with a list of topics to choose from for our first essays.

"Due in four weeks, on time," he said meaningfully, "and don't tell me about your dating problems, your hemorrhoids, or your grandmother's funeral."

I looked at the list of topics and panicked: "Medieval Iconography," "The Rose Window at Chartres and Christian Mysticism," "The Effect of Mariology on Church Architecture." I had not written an essay since high school.

"Presumably these topics will be clear after you've heard a few lectures," said Bert.

"I hope so," I replied, "because I don't understand the titles, much less have anything to say on the subject."

"You could go in and talk to the prof and ask for help."

"Not after the way he treated me in class," I said. "I'm determined to take everything he can dish out and do a good job. He expects me to be a dim-witted hausfrau. I'm going to prove to him I'm not."

My sculpture instructor "Ron" was the opposite of Professor Borges, but just as obscure. He strolled into our first class twenty minutes late. Giving us the peace sign, he plopped down on a table and arranged his bare feet and legs in a yoga position. I was glad to see he was wearing cut-off jeans—anything—under the poncho that barely covered his torso. He looked about two years older than Gail.

"So whatdya wanna talk about?" he said. Everyone looked uneasy.

"Oh, yeah, I'm Ron—"

A girl next to me raised her hand.

"Do you want our class cards?" she asked.

"If you wanna give 'em to me. I'm not hung up on 'em. It's what you turn out that counts." He waved his arm toward the set of pink tires and the lurching Volkswagen.

"Or maybe what you don't turn out," he said. "Maybe the best artist is the one that doesn't do a damn thing. I'm not here to violate your space or force you into my spaces."

"What will we be graded on in this class?" asked a boy. "Are we going to do a senior project?"

Ron thought a minute.

"If you can groove on a senior project, that's okay. Your Karma isn't my Karma—right?"

Ron put his hands on his knees, palms up, and stared raptly into space.

When class was over, the girl next to me said, "Does he want our class cards or not?"

My drawing teacher, Mr. Sanders, was young like Ron. He had trained at Yale, and none of us understood a word he said. He wore three-piece suits and a striped school tie and always stood up when ladies entered the room. He called me Mrs. Hoffman, helped me with my equipment, and offered me chairs in the tone of a Boy Scout with his first old lady at an intersection. His favorite word was "matrix"; "vortex" followed close behind.

Mr. Newman, who taught painting, was my best instructor. He was older than I, more the fatherly type I expected, and he had a serious though not ponderous manner. I respected him and his work; in fact, it soon became a habit with me that anything less than high praise from Newman could throw me into a complete funk.

Every time I saw Dean Pointer, he said, "Good morning, Mrs. Hoffman, and how are the children?"

Chapter 7

The first month of school was dizzying. I had studio hours to put in, Ron and Sanders to figure out, and piles of books on Chartres Cathedral to plough through. I used a dictionary as though I were translating from a foreign language.

Each time I thought I knew what Ruskin was talking about, Bert would come into the room and say something like, "Laura, I hate to complain, but you cut my sandwich on the diagonal today and I like it cut crossways."

Or Mrs. Meeker, the cleaning woman, would describe her ulcers and high blood pressure for the thousandth time. I already knew her varicose veins like the back of my hand.

"Would you climb up there and fix that drape pin?" she'd say. "I get dizzy on ladders and you know how my back is."

I was almost relieved when she quit.

I had an idea for my paper, but I couldn't seem to put my thoughts into words. Which point should I develop first?

"I can't *write,*" I wailed to myself. I probably needed Freshman English, but if I had to take it, I'd never finish my degree.

At my lowest point, when I had finally gotten settled with my books after chasing all over town to get a part for Barney's amplifier, Donald came home and put his books down next to mine on the dining room table. He needed a costume for the fourth-grade music program.

"You have to have a Japanese kimono," I repeated dully as he told me the news, "because you are a little Japanese boy in 'Children of Many Lands.' "

"That's right," he beamed, "and here is the pattern you're supposed to make it from—there are sixteen of us and we all have to look exactly alike."

He pulled mysterious-looking wads of tissue paper out of an envelope. There appeared to be eight pieces to the costume, including authentic kimono sleeves and sash.

"But, Donald," I wailed, "you know I can't sew!"

Donald looked at me impassively.

"When does this costume have to be ready?"

It was just as I feared: the 25th of October, the day my paper was due. I thought a moment.

"Tell you what—I am just not able to make you a costume—but we will go downtown and *buy* one."

I suppose I never really believed this tactic would work.

The next afternoon after school we drove to a costume shop. They had R2-D2 costumes, Snow White, Fairies, Miss America, Swiss Peasants, Skaters, Devils, and Angels, but nothing remotely Oriental. We tried another shop, children's dance supplies; they had tutus, leotards, waltz gowns, junior bikinis—no kimonos. Somehow I thought there would be dozens of Japanese outfits to choose from.

"I think what we want is a bathrobe," I said to Donald. "I used to have one that was exactly like a Japanese kimono."

"But our teacher said we were supposed to make our own—it has to be exactly like the others."

"How long are you on stage in this outfit?" I asked.

"I don't know. Amy says our cue, 'in quaint Japan' and we come on and move around and bow and take real little steps."

"Just as I suspected," I said.

"Do you have any Japanese kimono-style robes?" I asked the sales lady.

There wasn't one. Not anywhere. Not for sale, for rent, or in any size.

I decided to throw myself upon Miss Dewhurst's mercy: I stopped into Donald's classroom at College Hill School. All the Other Mothers, Miss D. assured me, were coming through beautifully. Not one had complained about the sudden assignment.

"But, you see, I'm a full-time student at the University," I said.

She stared at me with a profound lack of interest.

"I could do it for you," she said, "since you're so *terribly* busy. But after six periods of fourth grade each day, I go right home for my treatments."

She held up arthritic fingers.

"Whirlpool bath," she said.

There was nothing left to do but try to figure out that mass of tissue paper.

Glumly, I removed the layers of years' old junk from the top of my sewing machine which I'd bought because I was the only woman on the block without one. It took me an hour to thread the needle. It took me a day to cut out the pattern. I sat over my machine well into the night, straining my mind and my eyes, cursing Miss Dewhurst and the Other Mothers. By dawn of the 24th, I had what resembled a bad sugar sack with sleeves, one of which was backwards. I went to bed; I'd rip out the mistake in the morning.

Next day, before Donald could see the wrong-way sleeve, I ripped it out, and put it in frontwards. At last,

I had the finished product—it wasn't very good, but it was a kimono.

Bleary-eyed, I skipped classes and tried to get my paper for Professor Borges finished. I sat up all night again, typing with one hand, and drinking from a bottle of wine held in the other. Bert and the children were long asleep.

I thought of Borges's sarcastic remark about feeble student excuses as I rehearsed mine. I just couldn't face him with a story of sudden flu. If I told him I hadn't done my paper because I was making a Japanese kimono, he either wouldn't believe me or he'd think I was soft-headed. Would Rodin sacrifice his art to a kid's fourth-grade play? Borges was already in the habit of calling everything he didn't like in the art world "feminine."

I handed the finished paper in the next day, on time. I'd done a hell of a lot of work and secretly hoped it wasn't as awful as it might be.

At Donald's class program, I sat on a funeral parlor chair, feeling just that bad, and waited apprehensively for the Japanese number. Miss Dewhurst and the Other Mothers were chatting about how cute the pattern was. Then on came the Orientals; Donald's costume was definitely the worst.

On the day Professor Borges walked into class with his briefcase bulging and announced that he would return our papers at the end of the period, I perspired through the entire fifty minutes, unable to concentrate on his lecture.

"The north side of Chartres, alas, shows the gradual feminization of the Gothic, with its airier, more complex, weaker forms, and the true Gothic yields to a secondary phase—"

He was finished. He handed out the papers: "Steve," "George," "Mrs. Hoffman—"

I took my paper in trembling hands. Mr. Borges had not given it a grade but merely scrawled across the first page, "See Me."

Chapter 8

"It's that bad?" I asked.

"That bad," said Mr. Borges. He held my paper in his hand as we sat in his office.

I studied the spines of the art books in his glass bookcase.

"There is an idea in your paper somewhere," he said, "struggling to get out. But the writing is—well—abominable."

I was dying to blurt out all my excuses for writing such a poor paper—you couldn't make a nine-year-old boy the pariah of the fourth grade—the only one in Occidental clothes in a Japanese chorus. All my research had been done with punk rock vibrating the ceiling over my head, the television blaring, and Barney, Donald, and Bert telling me about their days.

But I refused to offer any excuse. Especially such weak, airy, feminine ones.

"What do you suggest?" I said.

"A little more thought and planning, Mrs. Hoffman. You seem to be writing off the top of your head—"

I thought of all those hours poring over books. Struggling with sentence structure.

"I suppose your household duties take up most of your time."

"Not really," I lied. "My family's been very cooperative."

"It would help to find a way to concentrate," he said. "Your paper is full of passion for the subject—of feeling—but it's not thought out. It's as though you were on five wave lengths at once. Or high on something."

He handed the paper back to me.

"It would help to learn how to use semicolons, too," he said.

When I got home, I found the living room empty, the television set turned off, the kitchen clean. There was something wrong.

"Donald," I called.

No answer. I went upstairs and looked into his room. There was Donald lying on his bed, staring dejectedly into space. Fluffy lay beside him looking equally mournful.

"What's wrong?"

"Nothing."

"Nothing? I don't usually come home and find you looking like a passport picture of Frankenstein."

He didn't smile.

I pushed a set of dirty sneakers aside and sat down on the side of his bed. On the table was a goldfish bowl with two fish floating upside down and a wad of chewing gum the size of an apple.

"Gee, you ought to clean up your room," I said.

A large tear trickled down Donald's cheek.

"Tomorrow—clean it up—after you feel better. What's the matter, now? It can't be that bad."

Donald handed me his report card from beneath the covers.

It was pretty bad. *B* in Math, but *F* in English, *D* in Social Studies. *D* in Science.

"Miss Dewhurst called me into the office for a talk."

I hoped she wasn't as mean as Borges.

"What seems to be the problem?" I said.

Another tear wriggled through the grime on Donald's cheek.

"I—I can't spell."

"Neither can I," I said. "Move over." I joined him on the bed and stared dejectedly into space.

"Gee, Mom, aren't you going to bawl me out?" said Donald. "You usually froth at the mouth when I bring home a bad grade—"

"No," I said, "I don't feel like it."

While I was fixing dinner, Barney came shambling into the kitchen.

"How was your day?" I asked.

"Boring," he said, "like all of them."

He opened the refrigerator and stared into it desultorily. He closed it without eating anything.

"You must have had a bad day," I said. "Anything special?"

"I'm thinking of quitting school."

My God, were these children psychic? I was just thinking that exact thought.

"Oh?"

"High school's so *boring*. So irrelevant."

"You have to go to high school to get into college," I said.

"That's just the kind of reasoning I'm trying to get away from—'you have to go to high school so you can go to college.' But what am I going to college *for?*"

I was just wondering the same thing.

"For anything you want to do," I said. "I sure wish I'd had a few years of college."

"But you know what you want to do—"

"No, I don't," I said. My voice got edgy as I scraped carrot skin all over the sink. "But I thought *you* did. I thought you wanted to be a movie producer."

"I did—but I dunno—lately I've been wondering—do I want to do that all my life? I mean, it might get to be a drag—"

"Producing movies?"

"Sure—"

"Well, still, Barney, I'm sure all the people you admire have had lots of education."

"Who—Johnny Rotten? He never got out of the third grade."

I let that one drop.

"Look at you, Mom, you had all those years of art school and now you're at City U. and you're just scraping carrots all over the sink."

Barney looked in the fridge again and slammed the door, sighing with ennui.

"I'm gettin' off the merry-go-round," he said.

As he left the kitchen, I read the sign on the back of his tee-shirt: "Goin' to Pot."

Was that an announcement?

For the first time, that evening, I worried about Barney. I worried about Donald. I worried about myself.

I went over to Judy's.

"I'm thinking of quitting my classes," I told her. "Everything's going wrong." I was near tears. "Donald's failing in school. I called Miss Dewhurst and she said he had not turned in his homework all year. Barney sounds—*alienated*. And it's all my fault. I'm so preoccupied with what I'm doing. That's why I've always done my painting in the basement. I was right there to be with the children."

Judy yawned. "Excuse me," she said.

"And for *what?*" I continued. "My own paper was so

bad Mr. Borges didn't even grade it—I'm an unfit mother and a failure besides!"

"Now wait—wait," said Judy.

I told her the whole story of the costume, the pageant, the research.

"Why did you ever buy that dumb sewing machine to begin with?" she asked.

"To prove I could do what other women do."

"You're not Other Women," she said. "Why don't we glue the top down and call it an end table? Or advertise it for sale?"

"And what about Donald? Let him be left out of the fourth-grade pageant?"

"Somehow I doubt that exact set of circumstances will ever arise again. If it does, hire a seamstress. Donald would be better off studying anyway than mincing around in the *Mikado*."

"I still think I'd better quit school," I said. "They must need me at home."

"It's Donald's homework," said Judy, "not yours. You turned yours in—alas. You can't do his work for him. He'll simply have to get on the ball."

"But if I had been home—and not abandoned him—"

"If you'll recall," interrupted Judy, "he was having a little difficulty in school last spring—*before* you 'abandoned' him."

She was right. I brightened up a little. But by the time I got home, I was down again and telling Bert, "I'm thinking of quitting my classes."

His eyes lighted up.

But when I told him about Donald's report card and told him how listless and peculiar Barney was acting, he wasn't so happy.

"Two *D*'s and an *F!*" he said. He smacked the yellow report with the back of his hand. "I can't believe it.

Donald has a perfectly good mind. In fact, he tested moderately superior."

Bert looked distressed. He listened to people's problems all day long and hated being confronted with them at home.

"We'll have to see that he spends more time on homework before he watches any television. As for Barney, I'll have a talk with him. I doubt that his 'alienation' is permanent and it may well be time for him to give up his Dracula cape and get serious. I think his shyness with girls might have something to do with this. At any rate, Laura, we've probably sheltered and protected the boys too much, not the opposite. From what you've told me, you went overboard running around on their projects."

I got up, relieved of the burden of guilt, and was about to leave the study.

"Wait," said Bert, "one more thing: about *your* using the boys' problems as your excuse to drop your classes— that isn't like you. You can't let one little failure stop you."

Now I was beginning to see why people paid Bert fifty dollars an hour for his insight. And sent him threatening letters.

"You didn't have to sit there," I said, "at the age of thirty-eight, and have a teacher tell you your paper is abominable. I felt like sucking my thumb and turning my toes in."

"My colleagues get you from behind," said Bert. "Some analyst from California said my article in *Psychiatry Today* was puerile."

"Did someone really say that?" I asked.

He nodded.

"I just wish I could spell it," I said. "Anyway I don't see why I have to learn how to write in order to paint and sculpt."

"You sound like Barney. Just be glad they didn't make you take math."

Bert set up a new regime for the boys: no more calling for Mom every time something was lost. The TV was off until all homework had been finished. Bert or I checked Donald's homework.

Many evenings, Donald and I worked on our writing together at the dining room table.

"You really can't spell, can you?" I said one evening as I checked one of his compositions.

"What's wrong with that?" he demanded when I pointed out a mysterious phrase.

"I don't know. What does 'Kerny Vents' mean?"

"You know," said Donald, "stuff that's going on right now—Kerny Vents."

Our new discipline for the boys worked well. I bought a grammar book. I began to feel a little more secure at school. I got used to calling people who were ten years younger than I "Professor."

There was just one person Dr. Hoffman hadn't gotten to accept my new way of life.

Each morning before I left for school, I made a baloney on white with mayonnaise and put it in the fridge. I wrapped it in layers and layers of foil, so the bread wouldn't be too cold.

Chapter 9

I felt in pretty good control. Until Thanksgiving. As the holiday approached, the picture of a beautiful brown turkey surrounded by red crab apples, bright green broccoli, and golden, spicy pumpkin pies conflicted with the images I had dreamed up for my canvasses. The usual feast would take at least four days: shopping, chopping, preparing the turkey, cleaning the silver, setting the table, making desserts. Maybe we could just get some carry-outs from Burger Chef.

But no, I couldn't do that. The family had always had the traditional things on the holidays. The children would probably not mind if we went to a restaurant, but to deny Bert a holiday dinner at home would be like stealing Tiny Tim's crutch. And where would Bert's father and sister go? They had always come to our house.

I was about halfway through the holiday preparations when Edith called and said she and Poppa couldn't come. Poppa had had a fall and wasn't feeling well, so we'd have to go to his house if we wanted to wish him happy Thanksgiving.

Poppa's house was just outside the city; it was an old, style-less frame hidden behind misplaced trees and unkempt bushes. Poppa was too old now to clip and trim, and he would never hire a gardener, nor let Bert do work that he believed he could still do.

We stood on the slightly sagging porch, ringing the bell again and again.

Eventually Edith came to the door, peered at us through the glass, and then recognized us. She was quite a few years older than Bert, and looked even older.

"I'm glad you're here," she said, "he's getting impossible."

She rolled her eyes to the ceiling and tapped her forehead.

The inside of the house was bare and cold. Bert's father came into the living room from the kitchen just as we entered.

"Poppa, it's so cold in here—aren't you cold?" he asked.

"Don't notice it," Poppa said, but he looked a little pinched and was wearing two sweaters.

"Do you mind if I turn up the heat?" Bert asked. "Poppa, it's all right to have heat in November—it's not a weakness, really."

He adjusted the thermostat. There was a fire laid in the fireplace, so he took matches from the mantel and lit it.

"There," he said, as the flames took hold of the kindling, "isn't that better?"

Poppa limped over to a chair and sat down.

"Did you hear about me and that damn ladder?"

"Yes—what were you doing on a ladder?"

"I was trying to fix the second-story window. Darned sash was busted and I couldn't get the window open."

"*Poppa,*" Bert said, "you mustn't try to do everything yourself. You've got to hire somebody to do things for you."

"They never do good work," said the old man. "They charge big prices. And don't do the work the way you do it yourself."

"I know," said Bert, "but a second-story *window*—that's dangerous. You're eighty-five—you've got to stop such things—"

"That's what I've been trying to tell him, but he won't listen," said Edith.

"Now what about that cough?" Bert asked. "You're coughing and wheezing. You want to come to our house for Christmas, don't you?"

"Oh sure, sure—I'll be there—this ain't much."

He coughed again, hard.

"Pop*pa*."

"All right, all right," said Poppa. "You'll be glad to know there's a doctor coming here today, any minute—though you can be damn sure I didn't call him—"

"Who did?"

"Her." He nodded at Edith.

Bert sighed and got up to pace around.

"I've been fine, Junior," said Poppa, "till lately. There's a fine-looking neighbor lady that's sweet on me. Brings me a coffee cake every other day. You don't have to worry."

The doorbell rang so loudly that it caused us all to jump. Poppa went right on talking. It rang again—you could almost feel it. He obviously did not hear it.

"Poppa, that must be the doctor," said Edith. She went to the door.

"I'm Dr. Brach," said the caller. He had a deep, resonant voice.

"Who is it—who is it?" asked Poppa.

"Your doctor," said Bert.

"Oh, *him*."

"Hello, Mr. Hoffman," said Dr. Brach; he walked over to Poppa's chair, so the old man could see him.

Dr. Brach was a pleasant-looking man—probably in his mid-sixties—gray-haired, a little heavy. He felt Poppa's pulse, examined his ears, eyes, and throat, and used his stethoscope.

"This fellow and Edith are in cahoots," complained Poppa. "Always getting together to discuss me—and run up bills at the drugstore—"

"Shh," said the doctor, "I can't hear."

When he had made his examination Dr. Brach sat back and lit a cigarette.

"I don't need no doctor to tell me why I got a problem in my chest," claimed Poppa. "I know what's going on."

"What's that?" asked Dr. Brach.

"My chest has been hurting a little ever since I fell off that ladder. One of my ribs is sticking into a lung."

Dr. Brach laughed heartily.

"Now that would be pretty serious, Mr. Hoffman," he said. "Actually, what you have is a virus, and I can give you some medicine to fix you up pretty quickly if you'll take it faithfully and not give it to the cat, like you did last time."

"You know that cat died, don't you?" asked Poppa.

"No—but even if it did—it wasn't from the medicine I gave you."

Poppa glared at him.

"You're right," he said. "It got run over. I just wanted to see if you were on the ball."

"Honest, Mr. Hoffman," said the doctor, "you *don't* have a rib sticking in a lung. I could X-ray you if you like, but you can take my word for it. Ask your son."

"Poppa, take the medicine," said Bert. "We want you with us at Christmas—"

"Doctor, don't you think Poppa ought to go to a nursing home?" said Edith. "He did fall off a ladder."

"I'm getting married!" said Poppa, "and then I won't be living alone."

Edith looked offended.

"You're not living alone," said Bert. "Edith is right here. But you might think about a good retirement home or at least an apartment; then you wouldn't have to worry about the house."

"I favor his getting married," said Dr. Brach. "But nobody wants some sick old geezer. So for her sake you'll take this stuff I'm giving you exactly as I say—okay?"

Bert and I walked the doctor to the door. There was no need to whisper; Poppa couldn't hear a word we said when we stood right beside him.

"Who is this woman?" I asked. "Is he serious?"

"Martha?" said the doctor. "She's a neighbor. She likes your dad—feels sorry for him. He's offered her all kinds of money to marry him. She could use the money, and a lot of women would consider it a good deal to exchange a few years' inconvenience for security. You notice how bare the house is. He's given her everything he owns as presents. She's returned every item to your sister. Edith has it all in storage."

"I'm afraid Poppa's getting senile," said Bert.

"A guy who can climb ladders and lust after widows?" asked the doctor. "He's not too bad. He is slipping, but mainly he's just bull-headed. Resists all change; but I imagine he was always a bit set in his ways."

"It's a family pattern," said Bert. "My sister's like that too."

"Your father's got to take a little better care of himself. He'll have to move out of the house eventually too, but not just now. I'll look in on him in a day or two—I'll call you about him if you like."

"Thanks," said Bert. "We live pretty far from here and can't get here every day."

"Happy Thanksgiving," said Dr. Brach.

"You too," we replied.

He was off down the steps and on his way to his car.

"Gee, what do you know? A human doctor," I said. "No offense, Bert, but I don't really think of you as a doctor-doctor."

"Oh, I agree," said Bert, "this one's unusual. Only Dr. Welby makes house calls."

We returned to Poppa, who demanded to know what we'd said about him.

"That you're doing very well—but *must* behave," said Bert. "Now let's take the first dose of that medicine. Let's see—one teaspoon now—another in three hours."

"Stop treating me like a fruit," said Poppa.

Edith went to the kitchen for water and a teaspoon.

"I still think it's my rib," said Poppa. "I felt it go in when I fell—think it punctured—"

"Poppa, the doctor said it could *not* be a lung!" said Edith, holding out the teaspoon of medicine.

"Oh, what in the hell does he know?" demanded Poppa. "He's just a kid."

On the way home, Bert was depressed.

"I'm going to have to spend more time with my father," he said.

I nodded. I was glad I had a Thanksgiving feast waiting at home to cheer him up.

♨ Chapter 10

I got one break by returning to school at my age. I made my re-entry into art just in time for realism, which had been "out" for the eighteen years I'd been away from the art world, to come back "in." In a big way. And realistic painting was my strong point.

"You can't imagine the contempt our professors used to put into the words 'subject matter' and 'iconography.' It was always 'mere iconography,'" I told Bob and the group at our lunch table.

"Strange," said he. The others, a girl with long blonde hair and a nun, agreed.

We four usually ate together. Bob, Sister Margaret, and I were the only ones in the school who could draw, and had formed a little clique and discussion group. Dora, the blonde, was dating Bob.

"I don't think you have to worry about your grade in painting, Laura. Newman really likes your work," said Dora.

"Oh, I'm too old to worry about grades," I said.

Sister Margaret gave me a piercing look.

"And I'm too religious," she said. "But I'm worried sick over what to do about Ron's class."

"I am too," I confessed. "I'd just like to think I'm

above it all—actually I've been walking the floor at night."

"I'm glad I'm taking graphics," said Bob, "instead of sculpture."

"We haven't done one thing in class," explained Dora. "We're supposed to be spontaneous."

"Therefore none of us has done anything," said Sister.

"He never gives us any assignments. Just talks about our Karma and says it'll come—"

"Well, something better come before the end of the quarter," I said, "and it hasn't yet."

"I *have* to get a decent average," said Sister Margaret. "The order is kicking me out in June and shutting down. At least you have a husband to take care of you."

"Yeah, I'm lucky," I said.

Then why did I feel so shitty?

"I think you like your friends at school more than you do me," said Bert.

There, I thought, that's why.

"Oh, Bert, what nonsense," I said.

We were sitting in the kitchen after dinner. We were growing more distant every day. Our sex life had gone from mediocre to worse.

"No, really," said Bert. "All I hear is Bob said this, Sister Margaret said that, Professor Newman said the other. And your eyes just shine when you talk about school."

"Not when I mention Borges," I said.

"Even him—"

I tried to think of a different topic to discuss.

"I think you're happier as a student than you ever were as a housewife," he said.

"Well, I just never had anyone to talk to about art."

"I guess I'm a pretty dull conversationalist."

"I didn't mean that."

"It's true, though. Artists understand each other, I guess. I've never been big on repartee."

"No one expects you to be."

"I'm fairly literal-minded and, I suppose, preoccupied with the mundane."

"Oh, Bert—"

He finished his coffee.

"Think I'll take out the garbage," he said.

When he came back he said, "Laura, did you know the filter on the dehumidifier is broken?"

"No," I said, trying to sound interested, "is it really?"

"I'll take it to the hardware store and see if I can get the part; otherwise we'll have to call a repair man."

"Um," I said.

"On the other hand," said Bert, "it may not be worth fixing. It's five years old and they probably have some new models."

I wondered if Ron would go for an ordinary representative piece of sculpture. To him it might seem new and strange.

"Just a figure, realistic, a person or an animal—till I get back into practice," I told Ron.

"Far *out*," said Ron. "It's so you. You're being true to your own inner space."

I think he was trying to tell me I was a big square. Nevertheless, our discussion gave me permission to get started on a project, and I assembled the skeletal wire structure.

"I'll need clay," I told Ron.

"What?"

"Clay. That's what you use to build up the figure."

Ron had never made anything that hadn't been either welded or sewn together. He was fascinated with my project. I think he believed the wire figure was the finished sculpture. He watched each step I went through.

My beginning got the other students going. My idea was so bizarre, it seems, it gave the others the courage to broach theirs. Ron liked them all.

Mrs. Goldfarb, a student who was actually older than I, had been closed out of ceramics and had chosen sculpture as the next best thing. She began doing something mysterious with clay. She did not build a superstructure but was rolling the clay out like dough.

"Mrs. Goldfarb is a horizontal person," said Ron to the class. "Her spaces are horizontal—compressed." Mrs. Goldfarb laid on with the rolling pin and glowed under Ron's benign gaze.

Mr. Rubel, an undertaker, claimed to be an advanced student and he brought in two blocks of marble that reached from floor to ceiling. These he began to chip away at with a small chisel. Later, he advanced to an electric drill with which he sent chips of marble flying dangerously all over the studio. In his long smock-coat and goggles he looked like the driver of a Model T. He worked on one piece of marble and then the other.

"Whatever is he making?" asked Sister Margaret. "They seem to be identical."

"One for salt and one for pepper?"

"Who writes your material?" she asked. "And what do you think of my doing a crucifixion?"

"Far *out*," I said. "So *you*."

Dora was up to something mysterious, too. It looked like a coat of arms of some sort; she was doing a clay model, later to be carved in wood, but her mind was seldom on her work.

"Bob and I went camping last weekend," she said one afternoon. "We had a great time."

"I did my washing at the laundromat," said Sister Margaret.

"And I had my sister-in-law for dinner," said I.

On subsequent afternoons Dora confided that she and Bob were sharing a loft: it was marvelous shopping for groceries together, magic taking stuff to the cleaners. Then, it seems, toward the end of the quarter, the spell began to fade.

"He won't tell me how he feels," she said. "He never communicates. He's all zipped up—emotionally I mean."

"Well—that's typical of the male, it seems—right, Sister?" I said.

"How would I know?"

"I forgot," I said, "but that sounds like the usual complaint. All my married friends say the same thing."

"I want him to go to a T-Group with me but he won't."

They have nonmarriage counseling? I wondered.

"There are some groups just starting for people involved in meaningful relationships," said Dora. "They have Jungian, Freudian, T.A., and Gestalt. I said he could pick—"

Gestalt would save time, I mused. I didn't see how Dora had the leisure to worry about her love life when she had so much work to do. Who was I kidding, I reminded myself. I wondered if Bert would go for a T-Group.

"Can married people join up?" I asked Dora.

"I don't think so," she said. "Only those with a meaningful relationship."

There was more truth than irony in her statement, I feared; relations between Bert and me had hit an all-time low. As he devoted himself more and more to his aged parent and his practice, I was getting into end-of-the-quarter panic.

My second paper for Mr. Borges was due, and I was working hard to finish projects for each studio course. I was more worried about my report card than about Donald's.

Mr. Newman was the only prof I could understand. He talked about color, shapes, getting depth in paintings. Mr. Sanders was still way out on existential interface.

A session in his class went like this: "Your drawing's accurate, Mrs. Hoffman. One only wishes for some acknowledgment of the—solipsistic. The nature of the act of drawing itself—the matrix of the creative moment."

Mr. Sanders's drawings tended to the minimal—just one or two well-placed lines with a passage from Kierkegaard or a Coomerswami poem printed neatly across the page. Why he needed Flo, our Rubensesque Cincinnati Dutch model for these, I'd never figured out.

I was sure Mr. Sanders would like Mrs. Goldfarb's drawing. She had deposited, as one might an egg, a small, wizened, miniature sketch of the curvaceous Flo right in the middle of her drawing paper. It truly drew attention to the act of drawing itself.

"Somehow," said Mr. Sanders, "you have missed the auchthonous quality of man which Flo so theatrically suggests."

Flo, who was stark naked and holding a difficult pose, yelled out, "Mr. Sanders, will you pull that screen across the door? Those damn janitors are peeking in here again."

Mr. Sanders adjusted the screen at the threshold of the studio that discouraged drafts and students not enrolled in the course.

"Erregtheit—that is the missing quality," continued Mr. Sanders, still studying the constipated form on Mrs. Goldfarb's drawing board. "A drawing is a rite of passage—a Quest—a resolution of appentence. The movement from profane desire to sacred transcendence."

"Five more minutes," growled Flo through clenched teeth. "I'm taking a break. Ow, my back. Get away from that screen, Henry. I see your eye in the seam and I can smell your breath from here."

I sometimes wondered why Flo, the most modest person I'd ever met, had gone into life-modeling at all. She was more like the suburban housewife with shopping bag than the model of Bohemian Paris. She went back a long way at the school. Maybe in the old days she'd been somebody's mistress. But Flo discouraged such speculation; her interests were fixed on the collection of soap coupons and cigarette package premiums she carried around in her ubiquitous reticule.

"Inwardness," Mr. Sanders was saying to another student, a hulking, not-too-bright jock named Crawley. "If the paper surface is a paradigm of the archetypal journey of man, then you have barely—planned your trip, as it were."

"You mean my picture's no good?" Crawley rubbed his hands across his face. "Jesus, Mr. Sanders," he said, "I busted my ass on this drawing."

"Cut out the profanity," called Flo. "Or I'm quitting." She knew life models were a vanishing breed.

"Sorry, ma'am," said Crawley, "I just got so pissed off I forgot there was ladies present. Mr. S.—will you sign my student financial aid card? And listen, I can't get here the next three weeks—I gotta tour with the tennis team."

Mr. Sanders paid Crawley no mind. He was studying the next student's drawing and commenting on the relation of the picture plane and the numinous vortex.

I redoubled my efforts with my second paper for Art History. I had to do better. I must master vanishing points and dangling modifiers, the flying buttress and the comma fault, transept and transition.

This time, instead of trying to work among the distractions at home, I did the research for my paper Saturday afternoons at the public library. There, I'd be able to concentrate.

I soon found myself queen of a little group of regulars in the department of art and music: the bums. There was a little old lady who looked like Bette Davis; when she wasn't at a table going through the stuff she'd collected in a canvas bag, she was in the women's restroom, howling. There were two old men who discussed the news like the hosts of the Today Show, and a heavy-set chap who made us all spring to attention when he blew his nose. It sounded like a long draw drape being pulled over metal rods. We thought the library was closing.

At his own table was a little old man in a too big, ragged overcoat who had been reading *The Philosophy of Marcus Aurelius* upside down with a magnifying glass ever since I'd joined the group. When you passed his table, a huge eye glittered above his books.

When I finished my paper, I felt regret at leaving the group; they weren't the intellectual companions I'd dreamed of when I signed up at the art college, but I'd miss them nevertheless. Until next quarter, I said to myself. I was sure they'd all be there when I came back.

After I turned in my paper, I waited for my grade with the usual fear and panic. On the day our essays were to be returned, I suffered through class in the familiar puddle of sweat.

"And so," said Mr. Borges, "as man began to take an interest in himself as an object worthy of study, the Middle Ages yielded to the so-called Renaissance and a new period in the history of art."

He handed out the papers. There were groans all around the room. I took my paper, leaving damp fingerprints on the cover, and turned to the last page where Borges put the grades.

"*Vast* improvement," he had written. "*D—*"

Chapter II

Nothing is ever so bad that Christmas can't make it a little bit worse. Holidays always brought out the worst in the Hoffmans, but Christmas was special: Bert's patients habitually went berserk with Yuletide depressions—then there were the parties, the presents, the visiting relatives, the Little Drummer Boy.

If I ever run into the little lad, I resolved, I'd break his drumsticks for him. Carols filled the air—in the bank, in the supermarket, in the season's most sacred place, the department store. Soon the Christmas spirit enveloped me: a feeling of panic, dejection, inadequacy, and despair.

By the time my classes were over, the holidays were just about upon us, and I not only had done no shopping, but very little thinking about a gift list. What free time I had was spent chauffeuring Donald back and forth to re hearsals of the City Boys' Choir Christmas program.

As I drove, I thought of menus, lists, and jobs to be done. With Barney and Donald home, life was one perpetual meal. Just when I could have used his help at lunchtime, Bert took to carrying his sandwich to the hospital in a brown paper bag.

"Patients going to pieces," he said. "Christmas blues."

Several days before the holiday, we got a letter from Gail saying that she would be bringing a young man home with her. "He wants to meet you. He really does," she wrote. "Please don't go to any trouble. Roy is at Harvard Law and very very brilliant. Please don't do anything special, just be yourselves."

"He sounds very broad-minded," said Bert.

"What does she mean don't go to any trouble?"

The next person I heard from was my mother.

"She can come," I told Bert.

"I better lay in some booze."

The week before Christmas I drove to Kentucky, where the Cincinnati airport is located. Mother arrived looking healthy and relaxed. She was the modern grandparent; still young and attractive, and she had all the accouterments of her breed: suntan, mink coat, a divorce.

"What have we got to do? What're you planning for dinner?" she asked as we drove home.

At last I'd get organized. The sound of Mother's voice would spur me to action.

"But, wait," I said, "you haven't heard the news: Gail is bringing a boyfriend home for Christmas."

"Oh, God—a great-grandmother!"

"Now wait—I said a boyfriend. She hasn't said a word about marriage."

"Why else would she bring him home? My Lord. I think I got the wrong things for the kids. I brought Gail a new Black Beauty book and Barney more Lincoln Logs."

We moved Mother into Gail's room.

"I'm giving Gail's friend, Roy, the den."

"Gee, Laura," mused Mother, "I can't imagine Gail being old enough to have a man friend. What's he like, do you know?"

"Here's his picture."

I found the well-thumbed photo easily in my purse.

Mother studied the features of the unknown suitor. He was dark, handsome, and wore a trim beard.

"He looks deep."

"Laid-back is the word," I said. "He edits the *Law Review*. He drives a Jaguar. He's twenty-eight years old."

Mother kept nodding her head.

"He scares me to death," I said.

"Oh, any boy would. He looks pretty cute to me. Now let's get going on dinner."

"It's only two-thirty."

Mother and I began our annual try at working together in the kitchen.

While I was cutting up carrots for stew, she took all the grocery bags that were jammed between the refrigerator and cabinet out of their nook, smoothed them down, and folded them neatly.

"Look," I said. "Those are for garbage. I save a lot of time by not folding them."

"How come you don't polish your copper-bottomed pans?" she said. "These can be quite chic hanging on hooks—"

Wait till she sees the silver, I thought. It was purplish black.

"I wouldn't dare put anything of mine on public display," I said. "But you know, now that I'm in school, I have to save as much time as I can."

"Well—you'll be out soon—right?" said Mother. "Don't worry. Then you can go back to doing things properly again."

By the time I sat down after dinner, I was exhausted.

"Mother's worn me out with one meal," I said to Judy on the phone.

"Wait till she takes you shopping."

* * *

Mother got my list filled quickly. Purposeful at all times, she pulled me away from items that merely caught my eye.

"We're not buying a diamond watch today, are we? Not for Charlie's daughter—she's only two—so why look? We haven't got anything for Donald yet."

What I was looking for was my own present.

What would I do with a white ostrich feather boa? Yet I kept glancing furtively at one as Mother looked at scarves.

"Do you like this?" I finally asked her, draping the feathers over my shoulders.

"You've got to be kidding," she replied.

Mother dragged me away from lawn furniture, thousand-dollar tea sets, bridesmaids' outfits—

"Just make up your mind. We have to finish today. We have to wrap presents and bake things for Christmas Eve. There's no use in asking yourself things like would Uncle Wally like a lamp with a ship model in a glass bottle for a base. It costs three hundred dollars. Just pick out a tie and forget it."

"But I feel that I should find something each person would like, even if I don't buy it."

"Don't be sentimental," said Mother. "Look—it's one o'clock—we haven't eaten, and we have to be at the airport at four."

"Oh, that's right."

I'd pushed the arrival of Gail and her friend out of my mind.

"Martini straight up," Mother instructed the waiter. She arranged her coat and purse comfortably in the restaurant booth.

"How is your *father?*" she asked me.

"He's okay. He'll be coming over for a visit on Christmas Day."

"Fine with me," she said. "I haven't a thing against him."

She ordered another martini.

"Not a thing."

At lunch, she began to lecture me.

"I never criticize," she said. "Never interfere with your children's lives! That's the first law of a sensible person. But, Laura, do you really think it's wise to try to get a college degree and run a family at the same time? Bert looks a little tense to me and you seem a trifle nervous. Something will suffer—"

"It's a lot of work," I said.

She looked meaningfully at me.

"You could have eaten off your grandmother's basement floor."

We have a dining room table for that, I thought. I never talked back to my mother.

Chapter 12

Mother and I were both nervous on the way to the airport. We talked of only one thing: the visitor. What would he be like? I pictured a Cary Grant type; suave, in full command. I envied Gail. Here she was running around with a movie star while I was living with an ordinary man.

"Gail ought to be able to get a decent husband," said Mother, as we walked down the long hall to the gate where their plane would land. "She certainly is pretty."

"She is that," I agreed.

"And she's bright," added Mother.

"Yes, bright," I agreed. Oh happy happy happy pair.

I was feeling old, old, old.

The TV over the window flickered and let us know that the plane we were waiting for was on time. We saw it land and slowly pull its silver snout in close to where we stood. My mother's eyes began to water and she looked like a little girl who'd lost her doll. I guess I did too. Both of us concentrated on the door of the plane that was now opening and the passengers who began to stagger out. Not them. Not them. Then at last, a girl with wild frizzy hair, a skirt almost to her ankles, and boots—behind her a shorter-than-I-imagined young man dressed in a gray suit with vest and carrying his overcoat on his arm.

They came over to us, and we were all speechless.

"What have you done to your hair?" I asked Gail. It was the wrong thing.

Mother hugged and kissed Gail and then I did too, but she was already mad about the hair remark.

"Mother, this is Roy Benson," she said, "and this is my grandmother—Roy."

Roy extended a firm hand to each of us.

Then we all stood there, sizing up one another silently.

"Well," I said, breaking the spell, "where's your baggage?"

"At the baggage counter, I suppose," said Gail tonelessly.

"It's down here," I said and we moved toward the entrance of the airport. I could not think of a single thing on earth to say to Roy. I tried to dredge small talk from my mind: How do you like Cincinnati? He hadn't seen it yet. Have you known Gail long? Obviously, if he was coming to meet her family. How do you like law school? Presumably very well or he would have taken up medicine. I dropped all the topics that came to mind.

We separated into two sub-groups, Mother and I hastening toward the baggage counter, Gail and Roy behind us. He had taken her arm proprietorily. They were talking too low to be heard.

The suitcases were moving along nicely on the conveyer belt.

I didn't say that. I bit my tongue.

The routine of pointing out the right suitcases, prying them away from the attendant, and carrying them out to the car gave us a language in common. Once settled in the car, however, the pall settled over us again. If only they would be a little freer with words, I thought. They seemed to be waiting for us to say something stupid, and then we did, out of pure panic. They're like a panel of judges, and we adults like Joseph K.—on trial, but for what?

"We'll give the den to Roy," I said, "and, Gail, you can share your room with Mother, okay?"

"My old roomie," laughed Mother. "Remember I always slept in the twin bed in your room?"

She could get away with comments like that.

She squeezed Gail's hand.

Roy, sitting in front, next to me, looked out over the hills and river.

"So these are the haunts of coot and hern," he said.

"Roy seems like a decent chap, wouldn't you say, Bert?"

"Nice fellow," he replied. "Seems quite bright."

We fell silent. Bert went into our bathroom and brushed his teeth and gargled.

"He's—nice-looking too," I said.

"Very."

I joined Bert and applied my several skin lotions.

"I wonder if I'll ever get rid of this stuff."

"Give it time."

"I've had it for fifteen years."

"Where did Gail say he's from?" asked Bert.

"Rye," I said.

We went around to our sides of the bed.

"What in the hell does she see in him?" asked Bert.

"If only he weren't so patronizing," I wailed.

"He's really hard to take," we agreed.

"Do you know he checked the wine labels at dinner before he drank any wine?" said Bert.

"And he acts as though he's in Timbuktu."

"He saw me reading in the study, and said, 'R. D. Laing—very good.'"

"He looks at Barney like something that crawled out from under a rug."

"That's understandable," said Bert. "But I distrust people under thirty who use pocket watches."

"He thinks an awful lot about food and wine for such a heavy intellectual," I said. "He rearranged the asparagus on the platter before dinner."

"Why?" asked Bert.

I tried to imitate Roy's pontifical style.

"Unfortunate to have *all* the asparagus pointing in the same direction."

"Well—we must give him a chance," said Bert. "And for heaven's sake, don't say anything against him to Gail. That's all she needs to make him irresistible."

"I'll try," I said. "But it's going to be a struggle."

"He looks like he's been reading *GQ*," said Barney. "Mr. Young Exec. On the Way Up. Favorite Scotch: Dewars."

"He's—I can't think of the word for him," said Donald. "It begins with an S—it means people who don't like baseball and never eat desserts."

"Slim?"

"No—soph-something."

"Sophomoric?"

"Soph—"

"Sophisticated?" said Mother.

"Yeah, that's it."

"Well, that isn't a crime," said Mother. "You boys are jealous; the whole family is. You're not being fair."

"Shh—keep your voices down."

Gail and Roy were still quiet but might appear any moment.

"We've all got to be polite—and remember our manners."

"I wish he'd remember *his*," said Donald. "He kicked Fluffy in the stomach just because she got a few hairs on his suit."

"Fluffy *is* shedding," I said. "I think you ought to keep her off the furniture."

"Mom, she's *pregnant*." He enticed our fat and flatulent dog onto his lap.

"Not at the table, Donald."

"I was just assuring her you didn't mean anything personal." He gave Fluffy a kiss on the head.

"I wish you'd be that nice to your brother and sister," I said.

"They're not pregnant."

I wish I were as sure of things as Donald always was.

"Should we wake them before we go on errands?" asked Mother. I shrugged.

"I'm no prude," she said, "but we oughtn't to leave them alone in the house, should we?"

"I have the feeling they've been alone before," I said. There was something about the way he brushed the hair out of her eyes and she took puffs on his cigarette.

"I'll see if Gail's awake."

I went to the open door of her room. She looked dead, face down in her pillow, hair streaming out over the bedclothes like a drowned woman. Her covers were all twisted around her and so was her nightgown. Her bottom was quite visible.

"Gail—Gail—c'mon. Get up. It's ten o'clock."

"Mph."

"Up."

"Go away."

"I want to talk to you."

"What about?"

"Get up and I'll tell you—c'mon—"

I went to the kitchen and reheated the coffee and cracked two eggs into the skillet. Gail liked fried eggs.

Then I knocked on the door of the den.

"Roy," I called, "how about some breakfast?"

No answer. Gail was up now, sitting on the edge of her bed smoking a cigarette.

"How does Roy like his eggs?" I asked.

"I don't know. Is he still asleep? I'll get him up."

She pushed past me, still dressed only in her nightie, barged into the den, threw her full weight on Roy, and said, "Get up—my mother wants to know how you like eggs." She bounced on top of him.

"What? What? Huh?"

Roy looked at Gail above him—at me in the doorway. He gave her a playful shove, and she bounced harder.

"How do you like eggs?" I asked Roy.

"Are you doing omeletees?" he said.

"I can."

"Get up then," said Gail. "My mother's cooking breakfast."

Gail bounced off the bed, still unconcerned about her appearance, and went back to her room to comb her hair.

Roy came to the kitchen to supervise the omelettes.

"Do you have any chives?" he asked.

I produced a bottle of dried chives, and he put a pinch of them into the eggs.

"Now just a dab of sour cream," he said, "and some mushrooms."

I started toward the fridge. I was determined to be nice to Roy.

"The canned are okay," he said.

While Roy and Gail ate breakfast, Mother and I had an extra cup of coffee.

"We're going out to see Poppa today," I said. "What are your plans?"

"We don't have anything special in mind," replied Gail. Both she and Roy were still disheveled and puffy-eyed.

"Would you like to go with us?"

"Oh, no. Not today," wailed Gail. "We're awfully tired; maybe we'll just go back to bed."

Mother winced.

Later that afternoon, we arrived home to a tense atmosphere. Gail and Roy and the boys had just come in, Donald and Barney from school, and the visitors from a shopping trip.

"They're having a fight," reported Barney.

Mother and I went into the living room.

"Hi, Gail."

"Hi."

"Good afternoon, Roy."

"Hi."

They sat on opposite sides of the room, Roy looking hot in his gray flannel suit, Gail with a hat jammed on her head, her long, colorfully stockinged legs stretching halfway across the room.

"Did you finish your shopping?" I asked.

"Not all," said Gail. "Will you excuse me if I go and wash my hair?"

She got up.

"Where'd you get the hat?" asked Mother.

"At Bloomburg's—do you like it? I thought it was darling and a good buy. It was only eleven-fifty."

She left.

"I didn't approve of her hat," said Roy.

I had to agree with him. It emphasized the Elsa Lancaster look of her frizzy hair.

"I said it was tacky and she's been mad ever since."

"Never tell a lady you don't like her taste—especially if she's got a bargain," said Mother. "The more you criticize the things a girl picks out, the more determined she is to have them."

I'd try to remember that, I thought.

"Gail's not usually so touchy," said Roy. "She's usually intelligent and reasonable."

Hm, I thought. As Gail's mother, I knew she was intelligent, but reasonable—no. People thought she was, because she agreed with them on issues that didn't matter to her, and she was a good listener. This gave her a reputation for being both tractable and brilliant.

"Well, excuse us while we see to dinner," I said.

"Quite all right," replied Roy, and he waved us away magnanimously.

"Well, I'll be!" whispered Mother.

Donald was at the table gobbling cookies and soda pop.

"Donald, you know you're not supposed to drink soft drinks before dinner."

"I was just finishing up a bottle that was already open," he said.

"I was just—"

"Gail and her boyfriend are having a *fight*," Donald announced pleasurably. "Ever since I got home they've been arguing and screaming. He's mad at her because she bought a hat he doesn't like, and she's mad because he's going to trade in his Jaguar and get an M.G."

"I'm glad to see their quarrels are on such a high plane."

"Yes—I don't think he ought to do that either—M.G.'s are dumb and Jaguars are *neat*."

"They cost a lot more," I explained. "Maybe Roy's doing the sensible thing—but it's not really our business."

Donald left the kitchen and I sat down in his place at the table. I bit absentmindedly into a furry pink marshmallow thing. This fight Gail and Roy had had confirmed my feeling that they were not ready for marriage —or anything. I sighed deeply. My elbows were stuck to the table. Soda pop and marshmallow cookies made a good glue.

"Excuse me, Mother," I said. "I'm going to go wash my elbows."

On my way to the bathroom, I passed Donald's room and glanced in. There were Donald and Gail sitting on the floor on Donald's sleeping bag, with ribbons and boxes spread out all around them. They looked about the same age. Gail seemed more relaxed and contented than I'd seen her since she came home.

Donald was her special favorite in the family. She had given him all her old horse models when she outgrew them. He called her "Rusty" for some odd reason, and she liked the name.

"Go away—go away!" they shrieked. "We're wrapping presents!"

When Roy came to the door there was more shrieking and shouting and gathering up of supplies.

Just before dinner, Gail came to the kitchen. She had taken off her hat.

"Mother," she said, "did you know Donald is quite upset about Fluffy?"

"Why?"

"Because she's *enceinte,* of course," said Gail. "The poor child told me all about it—he's been reading this horrid book all about afterbirths and hemorrhages and he's scared to death."

"Fluffy doesn't look worried," said Mother.

Fluffy was snoozing in the corner; she looked like a pregnant dry mop.

"Tell Donald I'll take care of Fluffy when the time

comes," said Mother. "I know all about these things. When is she due to have her puppies?"

"Any week now."

"Here's the book," said Gail, "and you better have a talk with Donald. He's like an expectant father—"

"I will," I promised. "And you'd better make peace with Roy. He *is* a guest."

"Oh, everything's cool," she said. "Don't worry. How do you like Roy?"

She took me off-guard by asking my opinion. It was such an unusual event.

"He's very nice," I said.

Gail looked into the pots I had on the stove. She added a dash of thyme to the carrots.

Emboldened by her softened mood, I said, "Are you and Roy serious, Gail?"

"Serious?" she said.

I waited in suspense.

"What a funny, old-fashioned word!"

She was gone again.

Chapter 13

Whatever happened to the woman artist, the one who was so involved in her courses at art school? I searched for her in dreams. But couldn't find her. Maybe she was the woman I was modeling in clay. But the features of my figure were not yet distinct. The holidays had landed me right back among the pressures that had turned me into Mom in the first place. I was back in my old role, preoccupied by Gail's and Barney's and Donald's and Bert's and Mother's and Daddy's and Poppa's and Edith's and Fluffy's problems.

I was so happy to see Sister Margaret, who stopped in to wish me a Merry Christmas, that I felt like kissing her. So I did. She was the only person I'd seen in days and days who thought of me as anything but Mom.

"Laura, did you get your grades?"

"Finally," I said. "I was getting terribly anxious and they came in this morning's mail."

"Mine too."

We couldn't wait to compare notes.

"Borges?"

"He gave me a *D*," I said. "I'm grateful. A zero and a *D*— don't add up that well."

"He gave you credit for class," she said. "You asked a lot of good questions."

"You got an *A*, of course."

"*B+*," she said, "but I'm happy."

"I only got a *B* in Mr. Newman's class; that's the one that hurts," I said.

"He's a tough grader," she assured me. "I think that's the top grade he gave. Dora and Bob and I all got *C*'s."

"Sanders gave me a *C*. I'm disappointed at how badly I did my first time out," I confessed. "I thought I was such hot stuff."

"I just hope I can land a teaching job," said Sister. "I've started applying for fall."

We never mentioned Gail once, but sipped glasses of white wine and reminisced about our teachers and fellow students.

"You took off so fast after the last class that you missed the excitement," said Sister.

"What happened?"

"Crawley ate Mrs. Goldfarb's still life."

"Next quarter's got to be easier," I said. "I think I can write a little better and surely—"

"Writing is so difficult," she said.

"I'm trying to simplify my life too—"

My mother came to the door of the sun porch where we were sitting. She wore a black-stained apron and was carrying a silver teapot.

"Your silver is just a mess," she said. "I thought I'd polish it up. Look at this teapot."

"I thought that was an eggplant," said Sister. "It's purple."

"Exactly," said Mother.

I introduced the two women.

"You sit still, Laura," Mother said. "I'll take care of the silver. Don't worry about a thing. If you'll just drive up to the store later and get some more silver creme. We're almost out."

"I still haven't figured out what Mr. Rubel is making in sculpture, have you?" said Sister Margaret.

"Not a clue," I said. "The monsters have very little shape and there's no carving on them—"

"Wait till you see Mrs. Goldfarb's creation," she said.

"What is it?" I asked. "When I left, she was crocheting something in pink wool."

"The flat part she rolled out like dough was a leaf," said Sister Margaret. "She painted that green. With the pink wool, she crocheted an enormous worm."

"So what is it?"

"A big pink worm on a clay leaf."

"Did she get an *A* too?" I asked.

"Ron gave everybody *A*'s. It's Christmas, and besides he doesn't believe in grades."

We drank to Ron.

"I'd transfer if I could afford to take something sane," she said. "But I need the *A*."

"I do too," I said, "and besides I haven't finished my figure. I'm going to complete it and then cast it in plaster when I come back."

"I wet the cloths on your clay model for you before I left," she said, "but you'll have to pop over next week and resoak them so the clay won't dry out. I'm going home —out of town—"

"I sure enjoyed seeing you," I said wistfully. "I wish you'd be around next week so we could go out for lunch. You haven't once asked me about my family."

"I wouldn't dream of it," she said. "I'm visiting my own next week and that will be enough."

As though on cue, Donald appeared for his ride to rehearsal, the new cleaning lady materialized with her purse and shopping bag, my mother reappeared more stained than before, holding an empty Wright's Silver Creme jar, and Gail came into the room asking, "Mom, where's the Scotch tape?"

"We're not allowed to ask that anymore," said Donald. "Mom's liberated."

"I can see that," said Sister Margaret. "Time for me to be off. See you next quarter, Laura."

Fluffy sniffed at Sister's heels as I walked her to the door.

"Starting a new family, Laura?"

"Not by choice."

"I see you're really streamlining your situation," she said. "I think you need assertiveness training."

After she left, I thought: She's right—that's just what I need. For Christmas. It would be a lot more useful than an ostrich boa.

Chapter 14

Sister Margaret's visit reminded me that I'd been hoping to do some extra reading for Art History over the Christmas vacation. While I was in the car making deliveries and picking up silver creme, I stopped at the library and got three art books. Maybe eventually I'd be able to remember what Quatrocento meant.

I was reading Ruskin's *Stones of Venice* in the study when Gail came in.

"Listen, Mom," she said. "Roy and I are going to run up to Chicago tomorrow. We'll be back by Christmas Eve in plenty of time for your various do's."

She was halfway out of the room before I called, "Now wait a minute!"

Gail looked impatient, as though dealing with a slow learner.

"Where are you going and with whom?" I said.

"Roy and I are going to fly up to Chicago. We'll be back in plenty of time for Christmas Eve."

"Gail," I said, "you're a freshman in college."

"So?"

"So you don't just announce you're going to Chicago with a man friend."

"Why not?"

"Well, you just can't. I mean—explain what you're talking about."

"There's a good jazz band at the Bizarre-Ritz. Roy wants to hear it."

"Where would you stay?"

"This friend of Roy's has an apartment."

"Gail, you can't do that."

"Why not?"

"You don't even know the friend, and besides—you know why not."

"Look, Mother," said Gail, "if Roy and I were going to do anything you wouldn't approve of—we have plenty of opportunity at the University. You can't supervise me all the time—"

"Of course not, but I don't have to encourage you to go and stay in strange men's apartments with a near thirty-year-old man. You're not a kid. Don't be naive."

"Oh really!"

She started out the door.

"Now come back here," I said. "Sit down."

Gail obeyed, but her face was set and she wasn't going to talk.

"Why does this mean so much to you?" I asked.

"It just does."

I sat on the couch, miserable. I hoped my lack of enthusiasm for Roy hadn't been so obvious that I'd made his and Gail's visit unpleasant.

"Has Roy been having a good time here?" I asked.

"Divine," snapped Gail.

"Then why the sudden decision to take off?"

"I told you. Roy wants to hear this band."

"That seems strange—to interrupt a visit—is one perfectly free to just leave?"

"Of course, he's free. We can't expect him to feel tied

here—oh, Mother—why make a big federal case out of it? It's a hundred-dollar plane ride. I wanted you to give me the fare—I won't have many other expenses—"

"I don't think so," I said.

"I'm not sure you can stop me." She stomped out of the room.

Almost as soon as Gail left the room, I had an attack of doubt. Had I over-reacted? I remembered what Bert had said: Don't criticize or disapprove. While I was wavering, Gail returned for a fresh onslaught. She was ruffled but trying to keep herself under control.

"Now, Mother," she said, "maybe you didn't understand the deal. Roy and I are not sneaking off for some sort of orgy, in case that's what you thought. We want to fly to Chicago for a concert. I have to know right away if you'll give me the money to go. We'll have to go to the airport and wait for standbys tonight."

At this moment Mother walked into the room with her freshly washed hair loose.

"Have you got a rubber band?" she asked.

I rummaged in the desk drawers.

"Here."

"What's going on?" she asked. "You two seem mad."

Gail threw herself into the armchair dramatically.

"I want to go to Chicago for the weekend to see a jazz band and *She* won't let me—"

"She means she and Roy want to go," I explained.

"Why *not?*" Gail said. "Don't you *trust* me?"

I looked at Mother. She didn't trust her either.

"You can't do that," Mother said.

"Why *not?*"

"It just isn't done!"

Now I felt on Gail's side. That was the kind of reason I'd been given when I was young.

There were different standards today. Maybe I was

being too strict. I'd gotten used to the casual way young people moved in and traveled together—from being around them at the University.

"You treat me like a kid when I'm home!" Gail said. "You *want* me to get into trouble so you'll have something to forgive me for!"

That was definitely something she'd heard in the girls' dormitory and was trying out on me. And something I definitely didn't feel.

She launched into an all-out attack, accusing me of all sorts of attitudes and feelings I didn't have, but which she thought I must have since I was a A Parent. My Generation came in for it too—with the neutron bomb, the Vietnam war, the oil crisis. Her accusations were more and more irrelevant. I'd been alienated from my mother when I was her age too, but at least I didn't bring in the world situation; it was because Mother didn't shave her legs and ground her teeth when she ate.

Gail finally got back to the subject: her trip.

"You just don't make sense!" she went on. "You and Daddy always said you looked at each case on its merits— you didn't pitch a lot of absolutes around—like 'it isn't done.' If you trust me, you haven't got one reason for not letting me go! Why are you so suspicious? So interfering?"

"I come from a broken home," I said.

She stamped out of the room.

I felt like a hypocrite. It didn't bother me a bit that Bob and Dora were living together, but I felt differently about my own daughter. I wouldn't object if she lived with a man she really cared about—in due time.

Gail didn't speak to me for two hours. Finally I went to her room. Humor hadn't worked to defuse her anger, so I tried logic.

"It would kill your father," I said.

"Why?"

"I don't know why. He's old-fashioned. He loves you. I'm convinced this trip is just as you say, and I do trust you. But I don't think Daddy will approve."

"You talk to him," she said.

"Oh, no," I replied. "If you're not to be treated like a kid, you talk to him yourself."

I went to the kitchen to check on dinner.

Donald came in singing, *"Deck* the halls with boughs of holly, fa la la la la la la— *'Tis* the season to be *jolly—"*

"Oh be quiet," I said, "I can't stand another Christmas carol."

"Well, you don't have to *yell."*

"I'm sorry," I said, "I'm just worried about Gail."

"What is she mad about now?"

"Oh—something she wants, and I said no." I bent over the stove, frowning.

"Mom, you remind me of Lucy in 'Peanuts,' " Donald said.

I forewarned Bert that Gail wanted to talk to him, and just before dinner, he sent Mother and Roy to a faraway pony keg for beer.

So then we were alone and could fight in peace. Bert and I sat down in the living room and turned on the news as we always did before dinner, when we had time. Presently Gail came into the room. She was stiff, formal.

"Did *She* tell you about my asking for the enormous sum of a hundred dollars?" asked Gail.

"She told me you wanted to talk to me—and incidentally a hundred dollars is a lot of money . . ."

"Here we go on the starving Asians . . ."

"You are so spoiled," I said.

"I want to go on a trip," said Gail. She took a deep breath. Maybe she suddenly realized that her particular father was not ready for her to go traveling overnight with a man friend. He wasn't enthusiastic about my going back to art school. I dreaded the coming scene.

"Can I go?" said Gail, "if I spend my own money?"

"That depends on where and when and with whom," said Bert.

Gail apparently didn't care if she wrecked the whole holiday for everyone.

Suddenly we fell quiet.

"Donald?" Bert said. He had become aware that Donald was nearby, eavesdropping. There was the telltale sound of a candy wrapper.

"Donald, are you eavesdropping again?"

Donald rolled out from under the loveseat. He had a comic book in one hand and a chocolate bar in the other.

"I was just reading," he said.

"You were just . . . ?" said Bert.

"Reading."

"Well—why don't you tell people when you're in the room?"

"I didn't know you were going to have an argument— I just thought you were sitting around—"

"Oh?"

"But then I couldn't come out. I was trying to be tactful."

"Do you know what that means?"

"Mom says it means shut up."

Gail was still determined and angry. She ignored Donald until he addressed her directly.

"Rusty, I don't see how you can go to Chicago," Donald said. "Did you forget about Fluffy having her pups? And me being worried about her?"

Gail looked struck.

"And my concert is tomorrow night," continued Donald. "Don't you remember you promised to come?"

"Your concert?" said Gail.

"Yes, tomorrow night. You promised."

"What's this about Chicago?" said Bert. "What's going on?"

Gail burst into tears.

"Why didn't you *remind* me of Donald's concert?" Gail demanded of me.

"Well—"

"I'll have to tell Roy a trip to Chicago is out of the question!" Gail said. She ran out of the room sobbing.

I looked cross-eyed at Bert.

"Will you explain what's going on?" he said.

"Later."

Donald rolled back under the loveseat, but before he disappeared he looked quizzically at me.

"You're a fuzz budget," he said. "So is Gail."

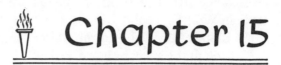# Chapter 15

The morning of the 22nd, I told the family I had to pick up some extra food supplies; then I drove straight to the University. It was like the old days when the children were little: I'd hire a sitter, dress to go out, then climb back in the basement window to spend a free afternoon sculpting or painting.

The sculpture studio was dark; Mr. Rubel's twin obelisks looked spooky. The clay forms were shrouded in cloths to keep them from drying out. I removed the covers from my figure and put them in the sink to soak.

The features of my clay woman were indistinct. I wished Ron were a little more experienced: maybe he could help me deal with the problem. Even her body was too—soft and shadowy. But I was going to teach Ron how to make a cast next quarter.

I stayed an extra moment after I covered my model. I sniffed the air. The smell of clay and marble dust and wood: delicious. I wandered into the painting studio. My landscape that Mr. Newman had liked so well was still on the wall; he'd put it up as an example of what he was after.

I was suddenly hungry and decided to have lunch. What a wonderful, wicked feeling: to have lunch alone without consulting three generations about time or menu. I crossed the street in front of the art school and found a table in Wolfie's.

"A Bloody Mary," I told the waiter, "and a hamburger."

"Through the garden?" he asked.

"Through the garden."

I enjoy having the family at home, I thought to myself, really I do. It's just that I also like sitting alone at this table with no one to please but myself.

"Hi, Laura!"

"Bob."

"What on earth are you doing here? I thought you'd be surrounded by your happy family—basting the goose or something."

"I do have things to do, but I came over to dampen the cloths on my model, and felt like lunch."

Bob looked dejected and even a bit pale.

"Sit down," I said.

His eyes positively lit up.

"Aren't you going to Pennsylvania for the holidays?"

"Naw," he said, "decided to save the bread."

The waiter returned to the table with my food and repoised his pencil over his pad.

"Yours?"

"Just coffee," said Bob. "Oh, and throw in a salami and cheese on rye and a piece of pecan pie with ice cream."

He looked at my sandwich hungrily, and when his food came, he began to gulp it down like a prisoner of war. He suddenly grew aware of my watching him and looked up sheepishly.

"Oh—first decent meal I've had since the cafeteria closed," he said.

"Why?"

"I've been saving. Pulling in the belt to make my expenses for next quarter."

84

"But you have to eat," I said, "or it won't matter if you make expenses. You look pale."

I sounded like a mother.

"Oh, that's nothing," said Bob. "Been selling blood to the plasma society. They pay five dollars a pint."

"Good God, Bob," I said, "selling your blood! That's ghoulish."

"Oh, it's okay," he said. "Look, let's not talk about depressing subjects. I'm celebrating with pie my running into you. Haven't seen a soul since our last class."

His face was taking on a slightly better glow as he put away his sandwich.

"I ran into old Henry the janitor the other night—half-pickled as usual. I was so glad to see him I took him up to the Anchor and bought him a beer."

"You must have been desperate."

"Right now I'd be glad to see Mrs. Goldfarb."

"Where's Dora?" I said.

"No depressing subjects," he replied.

I wouldn't pry, I thought. So I finished my cole slaw and called the waiter over and ordered a cup of coffee.

"Aren't you going to ask me what happened?" said Bob. He sounded let down at my failure to pry.

"Oh sure, if you want to tell me," I said.

I definitely sounded motherly. Sometime someone would want to tell me about their day, I thought, and I wouldn't listen.

"Well—she turned out to be a pain in the butt if you must know."

"Any specifics?"

"Oh really—she doesn't bear talking about. Stupid women are out of style. I must of been nuts to move in with her."

He pulled his pie over in front of him and began to devour it.

"Do you know what that mysterious sculpture project of hers was?" he asked.

"I often wondered."

"Her sorority crest."

"Oh."

I tried to cheer him up.

"Mrs. Goldfarb's was a gigantic ashtray shaped like a leaf with a pink crocheted worm on it."

"Mrs. G. is just Dora twenty years from now. Jesus God, I'm lucky to be free of her! She's got more hang-ups than Flo. But tell me what you've been doing."

"I haven't gotten a thing done," I said.

I started the tale of the family Christmas—beginning with Poppa's "punctured lung," which still threatened to keep him away from the festivities, Donald's rehearsals, and the unpopular suitor. At first I was trying to cheer Bob up, but then I found that I couldn't stop. I told everything—all but Gail's projected trip to Chicago: I told of my divorced parents and relatives.

"We've always had to have at least two celebrations of every holiday—at Christmas we have Christmas Eve Day and Christmas Eve and Christmas Day and Christmas Day Eve and the Burning of the Greens and the Burning of the Greens Eve Day and New Year's Eve and New Year's Day and—"

Bob was choking on his ice cream.

"And the dog is pregnant," I said. "She's moved into a D cup and I expect the puppies any day and Donald is traumatized—maybe for good. My other son wears a tee-shirt that says 'Disco Sucks'—which how am I going to get him to give it up when my father gets to town—he thought *The Agony and the Ecstasy* sounded like a dirty movie—"

I told him frankly my reaction to the suitor.

"He's nice," I said, "he's very handsome, very polite." I told him about the asparagus. "And then another night,"

I said, "I was cooking shrimps in beer for a treat; he went out and bought some Heineken's. He poured my beer off the shrimp and into the sink and put Heineken's on the shrimp!"

"The skunk!"

"Then my husband's sister is trying to get Poppa into a nursing home and Poppa won't move out of his house. He thinks this woman in the neighborhood will marry him. My mother is ironing the garbage bags and driving me crazy with guilt!"

Bob put his chin in his hand.

"God, it sounds like so much fun," he said. "I sure do envy you, Laura."

"Fun?"

I looked at him in surprise.

"All those people. Are you going to have a tree and everything?"

"Oh, sure—we always do."

I began to see my situation in a whole new light. I looked at Bob's dejected posture.

"I've got an idea," I said. "You come over for Christmas lunch."

"Gee, I'd love to," he said, "but won't that be too many?"

"How could one more matter?"

"If you really mean it, Laura, I'll accept," he said. "I mean, I was just going to stay in my apartment and open a vein in a basin of warm water."

When I got home, for some reason, I called Bert and told him what I'd done.

"Remember the kid I have the crush on?" I said. "I invited him home for Christmas dinner. Met him over at school."

"Oh my gosh," said Bert.

"He was going to be all alone at Christmas."

"That's terrible," said Bert, "but the thing is—I hope Gail doesn't sense what you've done."

"What's that?"

"Well, you've sort of picked the guy *you'd* like—as a substitute for Roy."

"Oh no, Bert—he just looked lonely. He's selling his blood to pay his tuition."

"That's what you tell yourself, but remember—the mind is always at work subconsciously."

"Bert, honestly," I said, "I wouldn't dream of trying to choose Gail's friends for her. Bob was just so pale and I thought—really, I didn't ask him as a substitute for Roy. Did I?"

Chapter 16

Donald was supposed to wear dark trousers, a white shirt, and a dark tie as a member of the boys' choir. All this I'd provided for him some weeks ago. But there was this person in Donald's life known as "some kid" who stole Donald's hats, tore his pants after one wearing, threw his jackets and sweaters in mud puddles, and in general was responsible for the wear and tear on his clothes. When I discovered that Donald's dark pants were torn at both knees, he informed me that "some kid" had pushed him during a four-square game. Same with the shirt. "Some kid" wrote all over his cuffs with ink. On the afternoon of the 24th, we had to run up to Barry's Men and Boys' Store and buy fresh clothes.

"Just be glad I didn't take the part of a Wise Man like the student director tried to make me do," said Donald. "They have to wear costumes and the Wise Men's mothers have to make them."

"How'd you get out of it?" I said.

"I told him my mom sold her sewing machine and bought a set of Ruskin."

"What'd he say to that?" I asked.

"Nothing," said Donald. "He's too dumb to know who Ruskin is—he thinks it's a set of storm windows or something."

* * *

The tie was a special problem. Donald wouldn't consider a clip-on tie, and all the others were long enough for a noose. They had to be tucked into his pants, and since Donald never zipped his fly, they hung out.

"Why isn't there something called a boy's tie?" I asked Mr. Barry.

He jammed his cigar into his mouth and claimed, "*This* is a boy's tie. Just a little long. Look—"

He wrapped the thing two or three times around Donald's neck.

"That's swell, isn't it, Donald?"

"No," gasped Donald.

"Well—make up your mind," I said. "Either wear a clip-on or this."

Donald looked frantic. There was no solution to his problem, and he was getting stage fright.

"I have a headache," he claimed.

"You have stage fright," I said. "It's normal."

It was my turn to take the car pool. I left the house before the rest of the family to deliver the boys backstage at the Music Hall. The others were to come at performance time, and I'd join them in our seats. Donald's director, Doc, was very anxious (he directed two hundred fourth-grade boys) —and insisted that the performers be a whole hour early.

In the car besides Donald were John, Gary, Harold, Howie, and Lester. The six of them sang, cracked gum, punched one another and yelled.

"Hey, Mom!" Donald shouted, "Lester *likes* that onion gum. Smell his breath!"

"No, thank you," I said.

Lester belched loudly.

"It's good!"

"It's supposed to be a trick!" screamed Howie. "It's supposed to make you sick, you *re*tard!"

The others all punched Lester, who took his beating good-naturedly. Donald's stage fright or headache seemed to have disappeared.

There was an agonizing wait in the catacombs beneath the stage. We were told to be quiet, stay together, and hang onto costumes and props. Doc kept running in and out, shouting, screaming, perspiring, and demanding, "Where's Miller?" "Where's Pleasant Hill?" "Where's Roselawn?" "Where are the altos?"

The room was hot, airless, and the boys gobbled down peanuts, candy bars, cocoa, milk, Cheese-Its, and grape pop—on top of the onion gum and dinner. I had Sartre-ish fantasies—this was like a *No Exit* vision of hell, and I felt tricked. I'd imagined a hell that might be everlasting and hot, but it had never occurred to me that one might be with one's children—or that there'd be vending machines.

Howie said he felt very funny. Lester offered him a bit of his nice cool fudgesicle, but Howie waved it away. He definitely felt funny—

"Howie, go in the boys' room and get a paper towel and wet it," I said. "Bathe your head and—"

But it was too late.

A disgusted John shrieked, "You didn't have to *aim* at the glockenspiel, you crumb!"

All I could think was: Be grateful. This concert had resolved our problem over Gail's projected trip to Chicago, and I hadn't had to make a costume.

At last it was time to line up.

"Altos here, sopranos here. Actors!"

The boys jiggled and jostled in line. Lester ran his finger across his throat as if to cut it.

"We're gonna be terrible!" said Gary.

* * *

From the audience the boys looked so different. By the time I found my family, the choir had taken its place on the vast tiers on the stage. Behind hundreds of boys were high school groups and, behind them, an adult choir. The boys looked very little, and from this far away, like angels.

"Which one *is* he?" Gail was saying. "They all look alike from here."

"He's the boy three blonds over from that row of spades," said Barney.

"Barney!" said Bert.

"No—no—Donald doesn't stand up that straight, and look how quiet that kid is. Donald wouldn't be that still—"

"I found him," said Roy. "Now look—make a plumb line from the fourth bunch of fringe on the red curtain—now over from the red-headed kid—isn't that him?"

"Too neat," said Mother. "Look at that tie—it's perfect."

"I found him—the one picking his nose—look—that's *Donald! Gross!*" said Barney.

It was impossible to tell. That did look like Donald with his finger plunged in his nose. Or no—was he the one scuffling in the last row? That hair—"

We were making an awful lot of noise, but the people next to us were doing the same thing. The man looked familiar.

I leaned over to Mother.

"Isn't that Poppa's doctor?" I asked.

Mother looked at the gray-haired man just beyond Gail and Roy and Barney.

"Why, yes—it's Dr. Brach—I talked to him on the phone yesterday—he called for Bert. Hello," said Mother.

He waved. "How are you?"

She couldn't answer. The house lights went out, and

the conductor came bustling onto the podium. In seconds the music had begun.

"I think I've found him," whispered Bert. "Count five rows up and three over—see."

"Shhh!" came hisses from behind us.

At intermission we chatted with Dr. Brach. He was with an attractive young woman who turned out to be his former daughter-in-law. His grandson was singing in the choir. They couldn't positively identify him from this distance.

"You have such a nice big rooting section," said the doctor. His family had shrunk in size—his son was in Florida and his wife had died two years ago.

The buzzer rang and cut off our conversation, and the lights in the lobby were flashed on and off.

"Dr. Brach, what do you think about Poppa getting out for Christmas?" said Bert. "I tried to call you back today."

"I wish I could say he's fine—he isn't completely. But I think he can go to your house."

The second half of the program really used the boys' voices and I listened to their singing with tears rolling down my cheeks. Bert held my hand.

"Now, Laura," he whispered, "would you have wanted to miss this, or any of our other Christmases?"

"No," I said, "not for anything."

After the concert when we went backstage to pick up Donald, the choirboys were flying around like sparrows. As a reward for their performance, they were being treated to cookies and orange pop by Doc. Donald and his buddies were gobbling, swallowing orange pop, and talking as fast as they could, reviewing the concert.

"It was a mess!" said Howie.

"Did you see Lester when he came in—he forgot to take his gym shoes off—a shepherd with Keds on—the queer!"

"I just knew I was going to say 'myrhh and franken-stein'—"

"Dag, boy!"

"How did you like my part?" Donald asked Barney.

"Groovy!"

"It was just wonderful!" exclaimed Gail. "Barney, you might improve your taste in music—if you'd take a lesson from Donald—take a lesson, period."

"I improvise, man."

"I know."

"Let's go," I said.

"Wait, let us go through the line one more time!" begged Donald. He and his buddies pushed and shoved their way back to the soda pop. Joseph and an angel tried to block them, but the unholy six were too much for them.

At home, it took Donald a few more encores before he could settle down.

"Now be quiet, Donald," called Bert, from our room. "It was a very nice concert . . ."

"Could you see me when I did my part with the cym-bals, Rusty?" Donald called from his sleeping bag on the floor.

"Yes, it was great; you came right in on time!"

"My son the cymbal-player," said Bert.

I went to sleep with the strains of the music in my head. And the sound of Barney talking on the phone.

"Yeah," he was saying, "it wasn't freaked out or any-thing—they did the whole thing like on key—it was *beauti-ful!*"

94

Chapter 17

I always got up early on Christmas morning. This year was no exception. I awoke at dawn, went downstairs, fixed myself a cup of coffee, plugged in the tree, and enjoyed my annual quiet moment. Each ornament had a history. I put some Christmas carols on the stereo. Even the Little Drummer Boy couldn't ruin my mood.

One by one they appeared. No one else slept late either. Even Gail and Roy and Barney, who usually had to be pried out of bed, were soon in place, eating doughnuts and waiting for the gifts to be passed around.

The gifts said it all.

Roy gave me a cookbook and he gave Bert a bottle of decent champagne. Donald gave Barney a record, "Johnny Rotten Celebrates Yuletide," while Gail presented him with *Dressing for Success*. Mother and I both gave him nice conservative oxford cloth shirts.

From Bert I got the usual little jeweler's box containing a pretty, feminine piece of jewelry. For the first time in my life, I looked critically at what he gave me. Would I really prefer him to give me a set of paintbrushes or a sculptor's gouge?

I gave him a new chainsaw for Michigan and a copy of *The Feminine Mystique*.

Donald received the most bizarre gift: a keychain from Howie with the greeting, "Merry Christmas to a Turd."

But there was little time to linger over the presents. Mother and I left for the kitchen where we had preparations going for a late lunch.

"Oh, my gosh," she said, "it's ten already—and where did all this come from?"

Barney and friends evidently had snacked last night: there were sticky glasses and soft drink cans all over the counters along with pizza cartons and bags. I should make him do the clean-up, I thought, but there wasn't time.

Mother scooped the cans into a sack and jammed the extra bags, unfolded, between the refrigerator and stove.

"Don't ever tell anyone you saw me do that," she said.

We worked hectically in the kitchen until one.

"Daddy'll be here in about fifteen minutes," I told Mother. "He's only going to stay for a glass of fruit juice so the children can give him their gifts and then he's going to his sister's."

"Fine by me," she said brittlely, "if he stays all day. Did you invite him for dinner?"

"Of course, but he preferred to go to his sister's."

"Still drinks nothing but grape juice, I gather."

"That's right."

She made it sound like a crime.

As the arrival of her ex-husband grew closer, Mother got more brittle. She took the grocery bags out of their hiding place, smoothed them flat, and folded them neatly. She looked at the clock. Checked her watch.

"He's late, isn't he? Didn't you say one-fifteen?"

I took off my apron and looked over the tray of glasses.

"Just like your father to throw everything out of whack like this," she said.

"He's only two minutes late."

At that, I heard the doorbell and voices: Barney and Donald and Daddy. Now I was the tense one. Oh my God, I thought, what will Daddy think about the Dracula cape and the dirty tee-shirt?

"Laura, your dad's here," said Bert. He came through the swinging door and picked up the tray.

"You're white," he said.

"What is Barney wearing?" I asked.

"The shirt your mother gave him," said Bert. "I got him to try it on for size."

When I arrived in the living room, my father was ensconced on the couch with Donald on his lap, Fluffy at his feet, and Barney next to him, looking angelic. I kissed my father. Mother and he shook hands politely.

"Guess what?" Donald was saying. "Fluffy's going to have babies."

My father looked away. Conversations like this always embarrassed him.

"It was very interesting!" continued Donald loudly. "Herman, the dog next door, got into the basement when Fluffy was in heat and he did a little dance."

"Really, Donald," said Bert, "you don't need to tell the details."

Donald didn't even hear him.

"Fluffy didn't like Herman. She kept biting him—but finally—"

My father held up his hand as though to ward off a blow.

"Don't mention the facts of life to your grandfather," said Mother. "He doesn't approve."

"Hmmm?" said Donald.

"Let's have something to drink," I said. "Daddy?"

"I'll have a martini," announced Mother.

"I'll join you," said Bert. He mixed at the bar.

While I passed around the juice, Donald continued his conversation about Fluffy's coming confinement.

"They *eat* the afterbirth," he said.

"Guess what, Daddy?" I said, "after all these years I'm going back to art school."

"Is that so?" he said. "Not full time, of course."

"Yes, I'm taking a full schedule."

Daddy looked puzzled. He turned to Bert as if to a parent to discipline his child.

"What do you think of it, Bert?"

Bert looked uncomfortable.

"Well, I—"

"You're not going in for that Female Lib stuff, are you, Laura?"

He made it sound like the Mafia.

"Well—"

Roy and Gail saved the moment. Gail came running in, gave Daddy a kiss and a tie, and Roy gave him a manly handshake. Mother would not let it rest.

"I'm very proud of Laura," she said. "I should think you would be too. It hasn't interfered one *jot* with her home: Look at that silver tray!"

Mother looked as chic and brittle as she was capable of— all the things Daddy loathed most in a woman. I didn't want to be the subject of a parental battle, just have a pleasant Christmas visit with my father and get it over with.

"I'd like another martini, Laura," said Mother. "If the women of my generation had had something interesting to do, we'd have been better off!"

Bert rose to fill her glass and knocked over the tray of glasses. Purple grape juice flew all over the rug and hit my leg like a cold needle.

"Oh, shit!" I said.

"*Laura!*" exclaimed my father. When he left, he still looked offended.

"Is it any wonder I'm such a case of arrested development?" I muttered after Daddy had gone. "My father has lived through two World Wars, the Depression, and Vietnam, and he's shocked because his thirty-eight-year-old daughter said shit."

"Your father was always a very strait-laced man," said Mother. "Though I do think you might watch your language in front of the children."

We worked a while in silence.

"I did everything humanly possible to save the marriage," she said. "I begged him to go to a marriage counselor, even, but he wouldn't."

My God, I thought, sounds like Dora and Bob. Was every age group in America having love problems? Mother and Daddy, Bert and I, Roy and Gail, Bob and Dora, Poppa and What's Her Name, Barney and Anyone, Fluffy and Herman! I wondered what Donald was up to.

"You're not engaged or anything, are you?" I asked when he came into the kitchen to see how soon we would eat. He had a large sucker in one hand and a chocolate Santa Claus in the other.

"To a *girl?*" he asked.

"That's the usual way."

"Ugh," he said. "I'm never getting married."

"Oh—you will someday, Donald," I said.

He looked as though I'd told him he had Legionnaire's Disease.

"Hey, Mom," he said, "that's the doorbell—want me to get it?"

"Not this time," I said. "I'll go."

It was Bob, bearing a Christmas-wrapped object and wearing a wide grin.

"Welcome to the Waltons," I said. "Come in. We've just had Grandpaw meets Fluffy's afterbirth. Next act—"

I swallowed my sentence. I just remembered, the next act would be " 'Kid' Who Made Pass at Older Woman Meets Husband," or, "Handpicked Suitor Meets Daughter and Roy."

"Sit down," I said.

Bert had been compulsively gathering all the gift tissue and boxes together and was kneeling on the hearth burning it in the fireplace.

"Bert, this is Bob."

Bert looked up suspiciously.

"Pardon my position—I'm getting rid of this mess."

"Oh," cried my mother, coming into the room, "I wanted to save those boxes, Bert—and all that perfectly good ribbon."

"Brought you a gift, Laura," said Bob.

Bert got up and wiped his hands on his handkerchief as I opened my gift.

"What *is* that?" he said.

He looked at the small, smooth, wooden stick.

"It's a modeling tool," I said. It was hand-carved and sanded; hours with a carborundum stone had gone into this tiny object. Bert looked from my face to Bob's. His expression showed a tinge of sexual jealousy, but even more, it betrayed puzzlement—at being left out of something.

Bob and Gail's meeting went off smoothly enough. I'd prepared Gail a little with my story of Bob's blood-letting and loneliness, and she'd simply said to Roy, "Mom's always picking up strays: whenever there was any kid in my class that got into trouble—no matter how much of a hood or a greaser he was—she'd say, 'Oh, couldn't you invite him to your Halloween party?' This one kid had mugged a teacher."

* * *

"Well," I said, "dinner is coming along nicely. We'll wait for Poppa and Edith and then we'll eat."

"Gosh, I hope so," said Donald. "I'm *starving*."

"What's that you're eating now, pardner?" said Bob.

Donald was licking the Santa Claus into a mousse with a grape-juice-purple tongue.

It took the whole family to get Poppa and Edith into the house. Poppa had gotten arthritic along with his other problems and it was difficult to get his legs to bend enough to get him out of the car. Barney held the car door while Gail twisted his feet this way and that. Edith stood by directing.

"I can do it, I can do it," Poppa said.

"It's getting icy, Poppa, be careful," said Bert.

If we took our support away for an instant, he'd start to slip.

When we had Poppa comfortably seated before the fire, he began to cough, and Edith produced his medicine.

When he'd had it spooned down his throat, he looked around and put out his hand to Bob.

"Young man," he said, "you the one I been hearing so much about coming to court Gail?"

"No, this is Roy," I said. I almost pushed him forward.

"Bob is Mom's friend," said Donald.

Edith was still checking the windows for drafts, arranging Poppa's cap, and fussing with his blanket.

"Oh, Edith, sit down!" said Poppa.

"Well, you know what the doctor said—go easy. Poppa, put that highball down! You know Dr. Brach said you weren't to have any stimulants! And no desserts. You have a touch of diabetes."

"I got a touch of old age," he said. "And there's no cure for it."

"What do you think?" Bert whispered to me. "Do you think he looks older?"

"Than what?" I said. Poppa looked terrible.

"At least his mind's still in good shape."

"Bert, I brought you a present," said Poppa. Edith was passing out Christmas packages to the children and they were deluging her with plastic holly corsages, boxes of chocolate-covered cherries, and the other things children give to their spinster aunts. "Edith, where's that present I brought for Junior?"

Edith produced a gift and Poppa waved her away. He opened it himself.

"You always were one for books, Junior," said Poppa, "and I found this in the attic. It's an unusual book." He handed Bert the first volume of an encyclopedia set.

"Everything in this book," said Poppa, "starts with the letter 'A.' "

He looked up at Bert proudly.

Just as we were sitting down to dinner, Poppa began to cough again. He turned pale and then fainted.

Edith and Mother jumped up from their places, and Bert rushed over to him.

"Stay back everybody—stay calm—"

He eased Poppa to the floor, put a hand beneath his head, and with the other felt for Poppa's pulse.

"Get me a blanket, Laura," he said.

He sent Mother to try and call Dr. Brach. We all held our breath and waited, trying to be cooperative and un-panicky until Bert could tell us if everything was all right.

Bert called to Mother. "Are you getting the doctor?"

"Yes—thank Heaven—wait a minute—"

We were quiet so she could talk.

"Get me a pillow for his head," Bert whispered.

I ran to our bedroom, and when I returned, Mother

was saying that the doctor would be right there.

"He was at home all alone," she said.

"Gee, I wish I'd known. I would have asked him to dinner." It sounded dumb.

It was snowing, and dinner was growing cold on the table, as Poppa lay cold and white on the floor.

"Roy, help me get him onto a bed," said Bert.

Our house guest lowered his fork and looked at Poppa as you might a run-over animal.

Bob jumped up to help.

"Aren't you supposed to leave them as they are?" Roy asked hopefully.

"No, you're not," said Bert.

Roy followed Bob's example and the three men got Poppa into the den and onto the couch. He began to stir, and color returned to his face. He seemed confused.

At this moment, Dr. Brach arrived. He looked angry as he strode purposefully to Poppa's side. Once there, however, he brightened up—probably for the patient's benefit—and held his hand against Poppa's cheek. Then he took his wrist.

"What happened?" he asked.

"He had a coughing fit—and then passed out," said Bert, "all of a sudden."

The doctor took some new pills from his bag, turned to me and said, "How are you fixed for extra beds?"

"Well—we can find—"

"Your father-in-law had better stay here overnight—maybe for a day or two," he advised me. "The weather is getting foul . . ."

"Fine," I said. "We'll give him this bed—and double up—"

"I'm not staying anywhere!" said Poppa. "What are you talking about? What's going on?"

"Poppa—now *behave*," shrieked Edith. "You *fainted*.

Right at the table—you looked ghastly! All green and funny."

Poppa looked a little scared, but he refused to be buffaloed.

"Oh phooey," he jeered, "I just wanted to see if I could get a doctor to make a house call!"

"Dr. Brach always makes house calls," said Edith.

"And how do you know if I came to see you," the doctor asked Poppa, "or if I came to help eat that dinner that's getting cold in the dining room?"

That galvanized the scared little group.

"Oh, Doctor, you must be frozen—a drink—"

"*Can* you stay?"

"Sure, I was all alone on Christmas," he said. "My grandson went to his dad's in Florida this morning. And ex-daughters-in-law aren't the same as a family. We can even have this gentleman join us. He's just a little light-headed from his virus—so if he promises to stay here a few days and take his medicine—we'll just step out there and eat."

I had the feeling Dr. Brach was doing all of this mostly for Poppa's benefit; still, it was nice to have him for dinner. He was a delightful companion. He kept a close eye on his patient throughout the meal, which Mother and I warmed up.

It was getting dark by the time we were having coffee and liqueur, and Poppa, probably a little dopey from the medicine he'd been given, had gone to bed.

"I'll stop in this week," said Dr. Brach. "He'll be better in a day or so. But he should stay mostly in bed."

Bert told him about the book, and Dr. Brach agreed that Poppa was definitely getting senile.

"I'm mad at myself for letting him out today," he said. "He will have to make a change, too, when he feels better. I just hate to see a good man go down."

*   *   *

Judy called on New Year's Day.

"Can you get away for lunch tomorrow?" she said.

"No—I—"

"Oh, dear, I had so much to tell you! Guess what I gave Steve for Christmas? A divorce."

"Oh, no!" I said.

"He found out about my cooking instructor. Came home when we were making cous-cous in the Cuisinart."

"Oh, Judy!"

"I'm keeping Millicent. We agreed on that. It's all okay, really. In fact, I recommend it. I feel like a new woman. We were getting in a rut. And how's by you? How's school?"

"I thought when Poppa got sick here at Christmas and moved into the den and I had to take care of him on top of the house guests and the holidays, that I had reached the all-time peak of domestic complications," I said.

"What made you change your mind?"

"Roy came down with the same virus and Gail and Donald caught it."

Chapter 18

"Aren't you going to register?" said Sister Margaret.

"What are you talking about?" I said into the phone.

Poppa was still in the den. Roy had been moved to Donald's room, Mother and Donald were in Barney's room, and Barney was sleeping in a tent in the basement. It was about time for the feeding of the invalids.

"I looked over the class lists and your name wasn't on any of them so I got worried," she said. "Aren't you going to register?"

"Oh, my God," I said. "Don't tell me I missed the deadline."

I told her about the holidays.

"Is it too late?" I said.

"For regular registration. Late registration is tomorrow —when classes start—you have to pay ten dollars."

"I'll be there," I said. "My mother is staying on and she can take care of things for a few hours."

The lines at late registration were just as long as they had been before, and I spent another whole day being sent from building to building. Only this time it was cold and slippery. Inside the Art Building. A water main had broken on the first floor and the students were skating around from room to room. The Physics Building, where we filled out our registration forms, on the other hand, was so hot the paper curled up as you tried to write on it and it stuck to your coat. Once again I wrote out my mother's maiden name and listed my parents' childhood diseases. I still didn't know if I had a Social Security number and couldn't remember the one I'd made up.

"Do you absolutely need this information for your files?" I asked the clerk.

She looked at the form blankly.

"We have to have the whole form filled out or it won't go through the computer."

"Where do you put this information?" I asked.

She waved an arm at a filing cabinet.

"May I look?" I asked.

"I guess," she said.

I found a folder with my name in the file; among other things, it contained last quarter's registration forms. I copied the information on it and handed it to the clerk.

"Presumably that goes back into the same drawer," I said.

She shrugged.

When I had paid my bill, I went over to the Art Building to see if my model had dried out completely and to buy some supplies.

I met Mr. Newman in the hall.

"I got closed out of your class," I said. I didn't want him to think I'd chosen to change sections.

"That's too bad," he said. He shrugged. "Computers— red tape."

He didn't seem too broken up at losing me as a student.

"How were your first-quarter grades?" he asked.

"An *A*, a *B*, a *C*, and a *D*."

"Oh, I'm sorry," he said. He walked away.

"Morning, Mrs. Hoffman," said Dean Pointer. He was wearing a muffler and boots. "How are the children?"

Mrs. Goldfarb was alone in the sculpture studio and jumped a foot when I came in behind her.

"Oh my God, Laura, you gave me a start."

"Sorry. What's wrong, Mrs. Goldfarb? You're so jumpy."

"Haven't you been reading about all the rapes and muggings on campus?"

"Well, yes—as a matter of fact—there were one or two incidents last quarter and something over the holiday."

"I'm not sure I'm going to continue," she said.

I looked at Mrs. Goldfarb's tired face, and was thinking: Gee, they don't want an old bat, with all these young girls around, when I realized, looking at her this closely, that she was probably about three years younger than I.

"I wouldn't give up for that," I said. "Haven't most of these things been at night?"

"Mostly," she said, "but someone grabbed a girl down in the basement of the Nursing College in broad daylight."

"The situation is getting pretty hairy," I agreed. "Where are the security guards?"

"They're the ones that are doing some of it," she said. "They picked up one on suspicion—another one was selling drugs."

Sister Margaret joined us.

"I've heard of the Faculty Feeler," she said. "Apparently he's well known and strikes regularly—but he's never done any real harm. This is different. They've set up an escort service for us. If we go across campus at night we're supposed to call a central number for a male escort."

"What if one of them is a mugger?" I said. "Where do they get the males?"

"Volunteers."

"Cool," I said. "I feel safer just knowing Son of Sam is on the job."

Mrs. Goldfarb was looking so uncomfortable, I thought I'd better change the subject. There were few enough women in the College of Art and we didn't need to lose one.

"I got closed out of Mr. Newman's painting class," I said.

Mrs. Goldfarb nodded.

"I did too."

"I've got someone named Saffron."

"Me too," said Sister. "And it's Ms. Saffron. She's the first woman ever hired by this college."

"I can't wait to meet her," I said.

At last I was feeling less lonely.

Ms. Saffron came striding into painting class right on schedule. She was a large, somewhat butchy-looking woman wearing blue jeans splashed with paint, a shapeless tee-shirt, and no makeup. She looked us students over contemptuously, glanced around at the studio, and said, "I can see we're going to have to do a little consciousness-raising before we even begin."

She strode over to my landscape that Mr. Newman had pinned to the wall.

"Before we can have any decent dialogue at all we'll have to get rid of this bourgeois crap!"

She yanked my painting down and pitched it on the floor.

"No more pleasing Daddy with traditional forms—ego-centered fascist *white male* stuff."

"What about us white males?" said Bob. "Do we have to change our style too, or aren't we in the dialogue?"

Ms. Saffron glanced at him.

"Please yourself, Mr. Charlie," she said. "This nigger don't give a shit."

Flo gasped. She was dressed in a flowery wrapper and awaiting posing instructions from the new professor.

"Comes on a little strong," whispered Sister Margaret. Mrs. Goldfarb was wringing her hands.

"Now—who painted the little number I just critiqued?" said Ms. Saffron.

Terrified, I raised my hand.

"I could've guessed it," she said. "I bet you were a cheerleader in high school, weren't you?"

"No, I just look like one," I said.

Ms. Saffron threw herself into the wicker chair with the super-sized back in which we often posed models. She assumed a Queen Victoria "We are not amused" expression. She stretched one blue-jeaned leg out and let her hands, both of which were encrusted with gigantic Indian rings, dangle over the arms.

"We're not getting anywhere," she said. "Everybody go up to my show in the Faculty Lounge. You'll see what I'm getting at. Whole new language. Woman has to use womanforms."

"Sounds like a sanitary napkin," I whispered to Sister. She giggled out loud.

"Like you," Ms. Saffron said, noticing Sister. "You've been ripped off by the Church—right? Say it. Tell it like it is. But use womanforms to paint. No more pig rooftops. No more chauvinist landscapes. Pudenda Power!"

Crawley raised his hand.

"What's a pudenda?" he asked.

Ms. Saffron looked him over slowly as if searching for a word that might be in his vocabulary.

"Snatch," she said.

The third male in the class blushed, and Flo had a choking fit.

"I'm not used to language like that!" she said. "The professors here are all gentlemen."

"I'm sure they are," said Ms. Saffron. "And who might you be?"

"I'm the model."

"Nude? Do they have male life models?"

"Not since Tony died."

"I don't think I'll be needing you."

"You can't fire me; I have a contract!" snapped Flo. She dropped her wrapper and got up on her platform. She might be modest about her profession, but she would be darned if she'd let anyone else put it down.

"Oh God," said Ms. Saffron. "Dismissed for now. Go see my stuff and we'll try to get it together tomorrow."

Our small class trudged up the stairs to the Faculty Lounge, rather chastened and quiet.

"You should have objected when she wrecked your painting," said Bob.

"Would *you?*" I asked.

"No, but she's bigger than I am."

"She's bigger than I am too."

"She wouldn't lay a glove on one of the sisters."

"Even one that looks like a cheerleader?" I said. "Where are you going?"

The rest of us were turning into the lounge and Bob kept on walking.

"To the Dean's office to drop Painting," he said.

"But you haven't even seen her work."

"I don't have to," he said.

Music—"Wombsong" said the album cover—rattled the pictures on the wall and kept the large plastic uterus that floated above our heads like the Hindenburg swaying gently. "She-It," "Womb-Wrongs," and "Crotch-Magic" were bright red on white rice paper (woven by the women of Communist China after hours in their hand-made factory) . "Medea-Message," "Motherkill," and "Her-mony" looked like medical slides in black and white.

"This appendix must come out," said Sister Margaret.

"That's no appendix," I said, "that's a womanform."

I had a perfectly logical impulse to follow Bob down the hall, but I didn't.

She would call me an Uncle Tom.

Chapter 19

There seemed to be a contest among the invalids to see who could call for his pipe and his bowl the longest and loudest.

"They make the lushes up at Rest Haven look good," said Barney. "At least they're quiet when they aren't flipped out."

"Who is that young man who's always in the bathroom?" Poppa would demand.

"That's Gail's friend Roy," I'd say.

"Why is he always in the bathroom?"

"He's sick too."

"What of?"

"Same thing you have."

"I know what I'm sick of," Poppa would say. "I'm sick of Muhammad Ali. And you can be damned sure that if I ever meet him I'm going to call him by his real name."

For this I had no ready response. Nor for many of Poppa's pronouncements and questions.

"Where do you go every day, Laura?" he said one evening when I brought him a dinner tray. "Why aren't you here in the daytime?"

"I'm in art school."

"In *what*?"

"In art school."

"At your age?"

I handed him a fork and tucked a napkin under his chin.

"Why do you want to do that—go to school?" he asked.

"Oh—life isn't just cooking and cleaning," I said.

"Cooking and cleaning is at least good for something," he said. He pushed the food around on his plate. "Needs a little more salt."

I realized who it was that Poppa reminded me of. Of course, Roy wasn't senile.

"You know, Mom, Poppa doesn't know me and Donald apart," complained Barney.

"I know."

Poppa was in the habit of saying in front of the two boys, "Now which is the one I thought so much of? The other was okay too—but he was kinda—" he waved his hand—"backward."

In addition to Cassius Clay, Poppa couldn't stand Princess Margaret or Gamal Ralph Nader, the president of Egypt.

"How soon do you think they'll be back on their feet?" I asked Dr. Brach.

"No time at all," he said. "Your father-in-law is just about over the virus. But we can't let him go back to his house or we'll never get him to sell it. Soon as we find him an apartment, sell the house, get him moved—"

"And the others?"

"Not sure. Has to run its course."

That evening, Bert and I proposed selling the house to Poppa.

He wouldn't even listen.

"I'll stay right here first!" he said.

Once again I thought seriously of quitting my classes or cutting down.

"No," said Bert.

"But you'd be happier if I were at home anyway."

"That's true," he said, "but only if you wanted to be. He's *my* father. We'll get some help running this hearse-hold—"

That did it. I wouldn't let him hire an extra hand.

"We can't afford it. We'll have two kids in college in a couple of years. My mother and Barney are helping."

On Saturday, Dr. Brach had some good news.

"But you'll have to talk Edith into it," he said. "She's cutting up pretty rough."

Bert and I spent the afternoon with her and Poppa, making plans.

"This neighbor that Mr. Hoffman is so fond of, Mrs. Ratterman, has agreed to live at the house and be a paid housekeeper if Poppa promises not to propose marriage anymore. This way he can stay where he's used to, Edith, and you won't be stuck with all that work."

"I can't afford it," she said. "I have to save my money for a long terminal illness."

"You don't have a terminal illness, Sis," Bert said.

"All my friends do." She made the ones who had been to the Mayo Clinic sound as though they'd gone to a finishing school she was too poor to get into.

Bert offered to take on the extra expense. I wrung my hands.

Edith still looked doubtful, but Poppa was jubilant and ready to leave our den at last. He promised not to talk romance with Mrs. Ratterman.

On Sunday, his new housekeeper, who looked as though she could play all the Valkyries by herself, arrived with

Edith. The two women swaddled Poppa in warm sweaters and caps. He looked ten years younger when they had him ready to go.

"Don't let him walk down that front step of yours," said Edith. *"Everyone* falls there."

Bert made a litter out of an old cot, but Poppa took one look at it and balked.

"Mr. *Hoff*man," said Mrs. Ratterman.

That was all she had to say. Poppa allowed himself to be blanketed, cotted, and lifted. Mrs. Ratterman held up one side of the cot, while Edith strained under the other. Both were weighted down with medicines, bags, and extra mufflers. I held doors and helped along the royal procession while Bert warmed up the car.

Poppa grinned down at me.

"I'm gettin' married," he whispered. "You wait and see. She'll get to like me. I believe in puttin' a woman on a pedestal."

We lowered Poppa to the car and tucked him in.

I went back in the house and collapsed from being on Poppa's pedestal.

Chapter 20

Clutching a new list of impossible paper topics from Mr. Borges, I raced home to relieve Mother from sick call. Ms. Saffron, who had been teaching what she called Art Herstory all week, made Borges seem almost lovable.

"How are the patients?" I asked.

"Coming along. Dr. Brach called—said he'd stop in later tonight—maybe let Roy and Gail go back to school."

"Do they seem so devoted now that they've shared a bedpan and heard each other vomit?" I said.

"No change that I can see," said Mother. "Give it time. Maybe it won't work out."

"The twosome I worry about is Bert and me," I said. "Between his concern about Poppa, and me running a hospital and being always busy with homework, we don't —communicate much."

"Bert's a doll," she said. "You'd better hang on to him."

"Why did you and Daddy get a divorce?" I asked.

She looked at her perfectly done fingernails.

"I don't honestly remember the exact reasons."

"You don't?"

"Well, he used to complain all the time that I made a grinding noise when I chewed."

"But you got the divorce."

"He used to call me Mommy when he talked to the dog."

"Bert does that—" I said.

By the time Dr. Brach came to make his rounds, I was yawning.

"I'm afraid Gail will have to stay at home a while longer," he said. "She looks peaked—I think she has a touch of mono. Roy's fatigue at this point is mostly emotional. He strikes me as a somewhat fussy young man who feels threatened if others are getting too much attention. Donald returns to school tomorrow."

As we talked, a faint whimpering came from the basement.

"Fluffy!" cried Donald. He was making a fourth farewell appearance in his pajamas.

We heard the whimpering again.

"Don't worry, Donald," said Mother. "I'll take care of everything if Fluffy needs help."

"Who's Fluffy?" asked the doctor.

I was too tired to explain. I wanted to go to bed.

"What do we *do?*" cried Donald.

"Nothing now," said Bert. "In a little while we'll go down quietly and see how she's doing. First let nature take its course."

Bert fixed the adults drinks and sent Donald to bed. The alcohol made me even wearier.

We waited about ten minutes, listening for more sounds from the basement. Soon Donald was back.

"We'd better go down now and see if everything's all right."

"I'll go with you," said Mother.

"Go ahead, but, Donald, remember—don't disturb her, and don't stick your hands in the box," said Bert. "This

118

is a difficult time for poor Fluffy, and she'll probably do fine if she's not frightened or upset."

Donald and Mother left; the three of us in the living room couldn't sustain a conversation. We strained to hear what was going on.

Pretty soon—another whimper, a growl, and then Donald and Mother reappeared, looking shaken.

"Fluffy's acting funny!" said Donald. "She seems mad. She growled at me!"

"I think something is wrong!" said Mother. "I really do—I think you ought to call the vet."

"At night?" I asked.

"You called me on Christmas Eve," said Dr. Brach.

"I'll go down and look," said Bert.

A few minutes elapsed, and he returned also looking shaken.

Donald looked as though he would be sick.

"I'm calling the vet," said Bert. "After all—my patients call me at all hours."

He strode to the phone.

In minutes he was back, furious.

"I'll be damned," he said. *"Doctor's* gone to bed."

Dr. Brach laughed.

"You've got to know this guy," said Bert. "He charges two dollars more for an office call than the pediatrician!"

"His waiting room is cleaner," I said.

"If that poor dog—" he looked at Donald. "Well, Donald, we'll manage somehow—get me that pamphlet they gave you—"

"Want me to take a look?" asked Dr. Brach.

"Hmm?"

"I'll go down and check her," said Dr. Brach, looking in Bert's direction. "After all, I'm not a specialist like you—I've delivered a few babies—I still do once in a while—"

Donald raced to the den to get his well-worn pamphlet, the one that pictured a dachshund wearing a maternity dress and eating pickles out of a jar.

We all followed Dr. Brach downstairs.

"Nice doggie," he crooned.

Fluffy gave a convulsive shudder and strained. We eyes were red and sad and seemed to hint that she knew us but would be obliged to bite if we came one step nearer.

The doctor squatted within a foot of her but made no move to touch her.

Fluffy gave a convulsive shudder, and strained. We expected to see a puppy.

"Is there bright red blood?" whispered Donald.

"No, no hemorrhaging," said Dr. Brach, "but it looks like a breech birth. If you'll get me some rubber gloves and a spoonful of sugar, I'll give her some medicine to keep her from snapping and I'll help her along . . ."

"I'm going to do those dinner dishes—we'll be glad in the morning that they're out of the way," said Mother.

"I'll help you," said Bert. He had never done a dish in his life.

I got Dr. Brach the rubber gloves and coaxed Donald into lying on the couch until something happened.

I sat beside him until he fell asleep. When I returned to the basement, Dr. Brach was regularly lifting puppies from beneath the dog. He'd puncture the sack and lay the puppy in the box. "One, two, three, four, five, six," he counted.

At last came the heralded afterbirth. It looked like one of Ms. Saffron's paintings.

Chapter 21

I had more trouble than ever deciding on a paper topic for Mr. Borges's class. Should I write about the Italian or the English Renaissance? How could I make a choice like that? I couldn't even decide what to name the puppies. I went to Mr. Newman's office to ask for advice on my paper.

"I think it would help to narrow down your topic just a bit," he said. He looked at me carefully.

"Also," he added, "it might help if you knew what you were after in coming back to school. What do you want to do with your degree?"

"I want to be a professional artist," I said. "Show my paintings and sell them. I might teach part-time."

"I thought you were going to say something about fulfillment and finding out who you are."

"So did I," I said.

"Art's a rough game," he said. "Almost impossible to make a living. No reason why you can't fulfill your ambition though, if you stick at it. But for heaven's sake, don't go in for the silly fads That Woman is promoting."

"I won't," I said. Why did I always feel like Benedict Arnold when I agreed with a man instead of Ms. Saffron?

In painting class, Ms. Saffron sat on her wicker throne; at her feet were Mrs. Goldfarb, Dora, and Tony Ramira, a new student. All the males had dropped out of the class and the atmosphere had become like the Temple at Delphi.

The true converts had taken up Ms. Saffron's themes: Mrs. Goldfarb was stitching together a small suede egg, as yet untitled. Dora's painting, "Rape," wall-sized and bright red, was the hit of the class. Tony was rigging up lights and found objects for "Third World Womb." It had a microphone in it that spectators could talk into, in case they wanted to react.

Sister and I decided to go abstract as a protective measure. We were experimenting with Cubist and abstract forms, but covered ourselves with titles like "Sisterspeak."

Ms. Saffron continued to attack my efforts along with my personal style.

"Too Junior Leaguey," she'd say, gazing, not at my painting, but at me.

"Why does she hate me?" I asked Sister.

"You don't sit at her feet."

"Neither do you."

"But I've been ripped off by the Church, remember?" said Sister. "Mrs. Goldfarb is Jewish, Dora has become a card-carrying man-hater, and Tony is a Chicana. These are all good credentials and this is a credential society."

"And a dues-paying one," said I. "I guess she thinks I owe—"

"No doubt."

"But I probably have to work twice as hard as she does every day," I said. "She goes home to a bachelor-girl pad and her Siamese cat. I go home to a sick ward, a half-dozen puppies, three children, a disapproving husband, a guilt-mongering mother, and a ten-room house—which I usually clean myself—"

"But you look like you're having fun," said Sister.

I grinned.

"I am," I said.

"That's a no-no."

"Did you ever think we'd get into anything crazier than Ron's class?" I asked.

"Not in my wildest Womandream."

☖ Chapter 22

"Call us the minute you get there," I said. I kissed Gail and she kissed me back.

"I'm sorry I threw a monkey wrench into your work," she said. "After all, I was the one who said you should go back to school."

"I never want you to be sick," I said. "But it did give me a chance to see a little more of you."

"Yeah—parts you haven't seen for years!"

The times on the flight schedule flickered constantly; Gail's plane was in and ready to board.

"Don't overdo," said Bert. "Mono can recur."

"I won't, Daddy."

"Say hi to Roy."

And she was gone.

Why did people think that becoming very busy with other things was a stay against empty-nest syndrome? Or even a crowd back in the nest? I still had Barney, Donald, Fluffy's whole litter, and Bert.

Or did I?

As our guests dropped away like needles off the tree—Poppa settled, Roy back at school, Mother returned to Florida, and Gail on her way East—Bert and I should have a little time for ourselves.

We rode home, just the two of us in the car for the first time in months, and didn't exchange a single word.

According to my fantasies, Bert should have driven straight to some isolated motel, ordered dinner and champagne sent to our room, and fallen upon me telling me how much he'd missed me lately. But he drove straight home and began laying out his socks and underwear for the next morning.

"Bert," I said, "did you ever consider driving off somewhere—just the two of us—and hiding away in a small hotel?"

"When?"

"Well anytime—like today, for example, on the way home from the airport."

"You have to go to school tomorrow," he said, "and I have to be at work. I have an eight o'clock meeting."

"Oh."

In the following weeks, when I wished Bert would grab me and carry me away, he was never around. If I called him, he was always with a patient or in a meeting. He never called me during the day. Nor was Bert a grabber.

His way of showing his interest in me was very non-directive, like his approach to psychiatry. He'd shave at night and yawn a lot during the evening. He was often in his pajamas, "keeping me company," while I worked on a paper.

Why couldn't he use a little imagination, I wondered—and be just a little more directive? Be like the Sheik: hoist me onto his charger and gallop over the desert to his tent? Some afternoon when I wasn't too tired.

To be fair, I sometimes pictured this: me a captive of the brute, enjoying every sodden moment of his ungentlemanly attentions. But when he was out fighting the British or marauding villages or whatever sheiks did, I pulled out a set of paints and some decent paper that was handy, and I dashed off desert landscapes. For these I got the Nobel Prize in the Humanities, while our lovemaking brought peace to the Middle East.

The climax of my fantasy was the appearance of a sleek woman in many veils: she had done all the ironing. When I looked into the overflowing basket, it was full of neatly folded pillow slips and shirts instead of the dampened, mildewing tangle that was there now.

♛ Chapter 23

My model woman in gray clay looked cold but stoical as I splashed runny white plaster on her naked form. The plaster went in every cranny of her body and gradually built up to a thick coat. It dried as it hit the clay.

"So that's how you make a plaster cast," said Ron. "I've often wondered."

Sister was holding the basin of plaster and her hands shook up and down.

"Far out," he said.

Pretty soon my sculpture looked like a mummy, or an accident victim swathed in bandages. The plaster was so thick, the original shape was lost.

"What are the metal things all around her for?" asked Ron.

"Shims," I said. "That's where the seam will be—this is just a form we're making now—right? Later we open it at the seam, scoop out the clay, brush the forms with oil to keep the plaster from sticking, and pour in new plaster—okay?"

"Gotcha," he said. "But how're you going to get her out of there?"

When the cast was thick enough, I took off my smock; the next day we'd do the second step.

* * *

"Hey, can you hold that drill for just awhile?" I called to Mr. Rubel. He was on a ladder ministering to his twin marble things. I had the plaster form open and had dug the old clay lady out of her shell. She lay in the clay bucket, dismembered and slowly dissolving. The fresh runny plaster was ready to be poured into the mold and I didn't want it filled with marble chips.

"Be an interesting texture," said Ron. "Why don't you go with it?"

"Uh-uh," I said, "this isn't nut fudge."

I poured plaster into the two halves of the mold and then sealed them together, again using the metal shims to make a seam. The hardening plaster felt warm, like a person.

At home, the puppies were running around the basement, escaping from their box, and sometimes even making it up the stairs. Donald had promised to do all the care and feeding, but he had school and homework to worry about and somehow I found myself after a hard day's casting, filling water bowls, cleaning spots, and rescuing puppies from beneath the washer, from the inside of a Hide-a-Bed, and from the lint trap of the dryer. Naturally, I complained, but Donald's ready answer, "Remember, Mom, happiness is a warm puppy," disarmed me.

I may have school problems, love problems, and a lot of work to do, I thought, but I sure do have the *cutest* children that God, Dr. Spock, and any mother ever collaborated on. I passed Donald's remark on to about forty people; none seemed to think it as adorable as I did, though Sister had the decency to laugh. Unfortunately, Ms. Saffron overheard us, and if there was one thing she despised more than husbands, it was children. I went down, if that were possible, in her estimation.

* * *

It took me two days to chip the plaster outer forms off the plaster lady inside the bandages. I tap-tapped very gingerly with a mallet and a sharp sculpture chisel—being very careful not to split the whole thing with one over-zealous clip.

"I'm going to pull Mr. Rubel's plug if he doesn't stop with that pile driver," I said. "He's going to crack this thing with one of those vibrations."

My arms began to feel as though all the nerves in them had died. But at last most of the outer form lay around the lady's feet and she stood free and clear—a plaster person. She was blazingly white.

"Amazing," said Ron. "It all worked out."

"The tip of the nose was the hard part," I said, retiring my mallet and chisel. "That has a tendency to chip off."

"Ms. Saffron ought to like it," said Sister. "It's feminine enough."

"It's not the result so much as the process," said Ron. "Process here is the whole thing. Could you do this at the show in the spring?"

I scooped all the plaster bits into the wastecan.

"I was thinking of submitting the actual result," I said.

"Whatever feels right to you."

"Plaster casts are kind of uninteresting," I said. "How about for spring quarter, I work from this and do it in stone?"

"Fine with me," said Ron.

"By then I'll be able to move my arms again."

The day I finished taking the cast off my model, I got home to find Fluffy growling at her puppies and the puppies throwing up in their bed.

Donald was lying flat on his stomach in the den watching the original Mummy picture. I snapped the TV off.

"You are supposed to be taking care of those dogs," I said. "There's a horrible mess downstairs!"

"I was just—"

"I'll bet," I said. "Now, c'mon. Get a bucket and some rags."

We cleaned up the mess and put the bedclothes in the washer, but the puppies kept on vomiting. They tried to nurse and Fluffy kicked them away.

Bert was still at the office. Why couldn't I ever be at the office when emergencies occurred? I called the vet.

Donald sat in the car with a box of six sick puppies on his lap, trying to keep them from crawling out of the box. Fluffy cowered under my seat trembling.

At the doctor's we waited for an hour, sharing the waiting room with a murderous-looking German shepherd, a senile parrot, and two angora guinea pigs. I stared miserably at a large poster depicting Heartworm.

"Puppies just have upset tummies," said the vet. "Poor little Mama's got her a case of milk fever; that's why she won't nurse. We'll keep her here a day or two."

I was skeptical.

"That means another trip and more expense," I said. "Can't you give her antibiotics?"

Both he and Donald stared at me incredulously. Not give one's all for man's best friend? Dig deep for Heartworm?

"My O.B. man flies in here on Wednesday, Miz Hoffman. Couldn't we just keep Fluffy till he can take a look at her?"

"Your O.B. man?" I repeated dully.

"Best there is. These little dogs can have more problems. Probably we ought to get Fluffy on her feet and then have her spayed."

I signed the necessary papers.

The puppies would go home with us, where we were to feed them milk out of baby bottles.

"Maybe a tiny bit of cottage cheese later in the week," the doctor added. "If they don't keep down the soft diet, better call me in a day or two."

"You're going to do this feeding," I told Donald as we stopped at the dime store to purchase a bottle and nipple. But we shared the chores at the dinner hour, for the little dears didn't take to the bottle and had to be encouraged by sucking the milk off Donald's and my fingers.

"I always heard that sitting on cold cement gave you piles," I said.

"What are they?" asked Donald. He shifted his position on the basement floor. They might be something like girls.

Bert worked late and missed the whole adventure. I was just beginning to doze as he came into our bedroom. Through my nearly closed eyes, he looked very Sheik-like. He was carrying a tray with two drinks on it, and did not lay out his socks and underwear but came straight over to the bed and sat down.

"Thought you might like a drink," he said.

I sat up and took the daiquiri he had mixed. He had put a slice of fresh lime in it. While Bert undressed, I sipped my drink.

He got into bed. His cheeks were smooth and cool. He put his arms around me. But my arms fell away from his neck like crumbling plaster. The nerves *had* died in them and my bottom was still ice cold from the basement floor. My eyes snapped shut. I must have gone out like a light.

☗ Chapter 24

Something must be done. Vitamins, I thought. I need more energy. I called Dr. Brach and made an appointment.

"I'm tired all the time," I said.

"What've you been doing?"

I told him and he rolled his eyes to the ceiling.

"You need more than vitamins. You've got too many conflicts."

"Conflicts?" I said. "You don't know *conflicts*. I am one *big* conflict. Maybe I should see a shrink."

"Then you'll be poor," he said. "Just learn to say no once in a while and hire a little help."

"I have help," I said. "I have a cleaning lady once a week, but she can't raise her arms above her head and *her* doctor won't allow her to bend over. Why won't you give me orders not to bend over?"

"Because you *can.*"

"I'll have a yard boy come spring, but he can't start the mower."

"Great. And who cooks and cleans and takes care of the kids after school or while you're doing your assignments?"

"I do," I said. "I do the assignments late at night."

"Why does the painting mean so much, Laura?"

I choked. My feelings would sound pretentious. I was

sure all his other patients were contented with their lives;
only I was conceited and presumptuous.

"Something to talk about at cocktail parties."

He let that pass. Just smiled compassionately.

"I thought Vitamin C might help," I said.

"Would you like to take Vitamin C?"

"If it would help."

"It might," he said. "Then again it might not—what do
you take me for?"

"A doctor?"

He looked me over carefully.

"Are you eating and sleeping okay?"

"Most of the time."

He wrote something on a pad.

"Tranquilizers," he said. "Use them only when you get
too tense—and simplify your schedule as much as possible. Use Reddy Whip on the pumpkin pie."

"What would Mother say?"

"How is your mother?"

"Fine—getting a great tan."

"I go to Florida myself soon," he said. "I recommend
you do the same. You and Bert get away alone. Relax.
Get some sun."

"Write that on the prescription pad," I said.

He did.

I folded the paper and put it in my purse.

"I couldn't possibly justify spending the money right
now—or the time. I already feel guilty about the tuition—
and my ironing is getting moldy."

"Put it in the freezer," he said. "What are you planning
for next year?"

"To work," I said. "I can't go back now to what I was
doing. I'd be bored—and besides I'd like to earn a little
money."

"I thought psychiatrists were all rolling in dough."

"Not when they take on as many teaching hours as Bert does—and anyway, no one can afford three college students at once—plus a nursemaid for Poppa."

"Carry on then," said Dr. Brach, "and if you get too tired, we'll just run a red flag up over your house and declare it a disaster area. Now, how are the puppies?"

"They're another reason I want to work. Fluffy's having a two-hundred-dollar operation and the vet says the puppies need their teeth straightened. He's flying in his orthodontist."

"Next—" called Dr. Brach. He clutched at his head like a mad scientist. "I'm getting a migraine."

☖ Chapter 25

Dr. Brach was right. I must learn to say no and to simplify my life. For example, I might have the energy to sit up after the family was in bed and do my assignments, but I didn't have the energy to do that and also face Bert's disapproval. A Victorian husband, he thought I should go to bed when he did—and if I persisted in staying up later than his routine eleven fifteen-after-the-news-bedtime, he'd join me, looking more haggard and put upon by the moment. I wanted to yell, "Bert, we're not peas in a pod! I'll go to bed when I'm ready!"

Instead, I took my tranquilizers.

Bert was a doll; my mother said so. Where would I ever get another doll? Especially with twenty years of experience in living with me?

I also felt he should learn to make his own sandwich.

Well, if I couldn't confront Bert, I could at least confront Fluffy.

"This operation better be a success," I said. "I'm not going to run a doggie convalescent hospital. And you can say good-bye to your children. I'm putting them up for adoption."

Fluffy actually looked pleased. Could it be that in nature the impulse to mother had limits?

I dreaded facing Donald, but it had to be done.

"Donald," I finally got the courage to say, "I'm going to post a sign at the University offering the pups to anyone who'll give them a good home."

"It's about time," said Donald.

"What? You told me happiness is a warm puppy—"

"Yes—*a* warm puppy," said Donald, "not *six*."

At school I tacked a notice saying, "Spaniel-cum-Spitz puppies FREE," on the door of the Student Union among the requests for rides home and the ads for various workshops and programs.

"Assertiveness Training—Planning Session—Noon—Bring a Sandwich."

The notice caught my eye. Wasn't that what I'd promised myself for Christmas? And here it was almost Washington's Birthday. I decided to skip lunch and see what it was all about. My doctor had practically prescribed it.

Our leader was a tiny, fragile young woman in blue jeans and what appeared to be a lifejacket. Her hair looked like Fluffy on a rainy day.

She asked us to write our names and addresses on a piece of paper that she circulated around the room. My fellow students included Tony Ramira and Dora.

"I'm Kim," our leader said. She looked down at our names and read them off—connecting each one with a face. She stopped with me.

"Why did you sign yourself Mrs. Bertrand Hoffman?" she asked.

"Did I?" I said.

"Yes—don't you have a name of your own?"

"I suppose I do—" I said. There were chortles from the other group members.

If I flunked Assertiveness Training—

"What is your name?" demanded Kim.

For just a second I honestly couldn't remember.

"Laura Hoffman," I said. "You see—"

"Never apologize, never explain," snapped Kim. "Now first what we've gotta do is set up our meeting time. We want a time as convenient as possible for everyone. I guess you all have classes in the afternoon."

"Three thirty's the earliest I can get there," said Tony.

"Same here," said Dora.

The rest nodded.

"Laura?" said Kim.

"Well—go ahead if it's a good time for everyone else. I—"

Kim looked at the others.

"Why can't you make three thirty?" she asked.

"My kids get home from school."

"Are they going to melt if you aren't there one day?"

"Well, no—but there are music lessons two days a week and—"

"How about evenings?" said Kim.

"Monday's out," said a young man. "I bowl Mondays."

I would never have offered a flimsy excuse like that.

"My sorority meets on Fridays," said Dora. "We're only allowed two skips and I've had mine."

Or that.

Another student took a class Tuesdays and Thursdays.

"That leaves Wednesday—how's Wednesday for everybody?"

The others all nodded their heads, and so I did too.

I could change my night to visit Poppa by driving myself to his house instead of going with Bert. I took a tranquilizer. Without water.

Bert didn't like the idea of my driving alone at night.

"I'll be okay," I said. "Millions of woman have done it."

I couldn't believe the sound of my voice using a line from

A Doll's House. I'd never thought of myself as needing liberation; yet here I was slamming doors all over the place.

"If it's assertiveness training, Laura, why didn't you get the night changed?"

"I'd already said I couldn't come in the afternoon and anyway if I could throw my weight around, I wouldn't need the course—right?"

"I think you ought to be teaching it."

"Oh—how can you say that?" I asked.

"Well, here I am sitting alone another night of the week—that makes two—one while you become assertive and one while you visit relatives—"

"*Your* father," I reminded him.

"I'm still alone," he said. He looked disapproving. But Bert was nothing if not nondirective.

"Be sure you lock your car doors," he said.

The subject was dropped. Temporarily. Bert put his pajamas on while I was propped up in bed studying a book for my paper for Borges.

"What will you do if you get a flat?" he said, sticking his head around the bathroom door. "It's mostly country on the way to Poppa's—there aren't a lot of gas stations."

I could just see myself with a flat, alone in the dark: I flag down a car. It just happens to be a mugger with rape on his mind—the one terrorizing the campus. He'd noticed me at the University and been following me day and night, waiting for a moment like this. I was ready to give up my class. Then I wondered what Bert would do if he had a flat. He couldn't change a tire either. And if the mugger had a knife, his size wouldn't be much help.

"Do you know where the distress signal on the car is?" Bert asked.

"No—I didn't know there was one."

Bert insisted on taking me to the garage and showing

me the gadget on the steering wheel that I could flick on if I had any car trouble.

"You just put this on and sit tight in the car till the highway patrol comes along," he said.

I tried it myself.

"You might need it going to that night class, too," he said.

I turned around to hug him but he was gone.

"You're a doll," I told the empty seat. "Because you hate what I'm doing but are trying to go along with it and also trying to think of my safety and not just flexing your muscles."

But he was never there to hear me when I had something nice to say—and he hadn't brought drinks to bed since the night I fell asleep at the wrong moment. I raced upstairs to find him; I wasn't a bit tired this evening.

"Rhett, Rhett!" I called through the fog.

But his light was out. He had deposited my books in the study.

When report cards came home, tensions grew. Donald had not improved; in fact, his spelling was worse than it had been. And our policy with Barney had failed too. He continued to wear the Dracula outfit and his tee-shirt had become filthier in every way.

"Are you making sure Donald does his homework?" asked Bert.

"Positive."

"Barney's is a mild identity crisis," he said, "not atypical of adolescents. But the confusion he feels is made worse by today's situation where there is no clear-cut definition between male and female roles."

He wasn't naming any names, mind you, but it sounded as though I were to blame.

"With all due respect to the women's movement, it has

created a muddled situation for the young person trying to grow up and assume a place in society. Barney just can't decide if he wants to date, to take on the responsibilities of a grown male—"

"So he's thinking of becoming a *vampire bat?*"

"Not literally, Laura, of course—this outlandish costume is simply a protection from adult decisions."

"I suppose it's my fault—"

"Well, it doesn't matter whose fault it is—"

He didn't say it wasn't my fault.

Miss Scarlett was mad now, and was not at home to Captain Butler.

Chapter 26

That very evening was the first session of my Assertiveness Training Group.

"I'm going to be a few minutes late getting home," I told Bert. "Mr. Borges said he'd be in his office from eight to nine and I'm dropping off my late paper after class."

"I'll be at Poppa's," he replied. "But I'll leave the garage door open for you."

I realized as I drove to the University how little I'd been out at night alone. I had never traveled alone—never been away from Bert for a single night for twenty years. This assertiveness course was long overdue.

"Where do you get your money?" Kim asked the class.

"What money?" said Tony.

"My parents," said Dora.

The others had similar confessions to make, while a few were self-supporting.

"Laura?" asked Kim, "where do you get *your* money?"

"Out of a box," I replied. I blushed.

"A box?"

"In my husband's top dresser drawer."

"Do you keep all the family's money there?"

"Just household cash."

"Well, what about your bank account? Insurance?"

"My husband does all the bookkeeping. I don't really know—"

It certainly sounded feeble. I had to endure the stares of the group.

"It is very difficult to achieve true personhood when you have no control over your finances," said Kim. "In a materialistic society like ours, where the only reward worth having is money, one must have assets of one's own and make the decisions about how they shall be spent or invested."

"My husband would kill me if I tried to interfere in runnin' our finances," said Tony. "He already says I'm tryin' to steal his balls by comin' to school."

"Are any of you women in the group insured?" asked Kim.

We looked at one another. It had never occurred to us that we should be. What were we worth?

"If you died, your husbands would have to hire about four people to take over your household jobs—right?"

"Good point," I muttered.

"But what about me?" said Dora. "My parents wouldn't have to hire a new daughter. I really am worthless."

"Nonsense," said one of the men in the group.

"Dora, of course you're not worthless," I said.

"What good am I?" she demanded.

I couldn't think of an answer.

"All human beings are worthy," said Kim. "You don't have to justify your existence. Now, before you can start learning to assert yourselves, you have to believe that—right?"

"It ain't gonna be easy," said the man I knew only as Fred, "with your wife telling you what a shit you are all the time."

"An' your husban' puttin' you down," added Tony.

At the stroke of eight-thirty, I took my purse off the

back of my chair and began to gather myself together to depart.

"How many wanna go another half hour?" asked Kim.

Everyone but me raised his hand.

"Laura—you got more music lessons?"

"No—I have to turn in a late paper to my art history prof."

"What's the matter, you don't see him in class tomorrow?"

"Well—actually I do. But he gave me an extension till tonight only—so I thought—"

"Can one day make a difference to him?"

The rest of the group looked challenging along with Kim.

"I thought he was nice to extend the time at all—"

"Nice—nice—that word's gotta go. More harm done by Mr. Nice Guy than all the ordinary folks in the world—"

I wavered like a rabbit whose nest is invaded. I was going to have to be assertive with Borges or with this group. I was more afraid of him, so I got up and walked to the door.

"I promised," I said.

It was very dark out and I had to walk across campus to get to the Art Building, so I picked up the red phone in the Student Union and called the escort service. I felt silly, but even the student paper had recommended that women use it at night. I waited in the nearly empty, cigarette-butt-strewn lounge for about twenty minutes. At last, a small chunky young man with the eyes of a maniac appeared at my side and said, "Mrs. Hoffman?" I stood up.

I noticed that the young man bit his nails way down past the quick.

"What's your name?" I said.

"Joe."

Joe was pathologically quiet. I could not coax another word out of him. Just my luck, I thought. I knew it. I could see the headline and newspaper story: Escort Service Provides Killer to "Protect" the Late Mrs. Laura Hoffman. A strange twist of fate . . . a model young man . . . straight *A* student . . . always quiet, obedient . . . loved his mother.

"Do you live at home or in the dorm?" I asked Joe.

"Home," said he. "Just me and my mom."

We entered a deserted stairwell that took us through the science labs to the Art Building: three floors of twisty, cement labyrinth filled with paper cups, cigarette butts, and sandwich wrappers. The administration had provided for one's safety by posting a clearly stated warning that "Only students and staff of the University may use this exit."

Terrific, I thought.

By the time I got to the Art Building I was frantic to get away from Joe and his murderous eyes. The light in Mr. Borges's office and the smell of coffee beckoned toward safety.

"Thanks, Joe," I said. "After my appointment, I can get to my car from here."

"Take it easy," he said.

With relief I waved good-bye.

"Coffee?" said Mr. Borges, coming to the door of his office.

"Yes, thanks."

I sat down and gratefully cuddled a mug of coffee.

"How did the research go this time?" asked Borges.

"I think it's better." I remembered my assertiveness session. "I even think it's good. I didn't realize there were so many good genre painters outside the big names I'd heard of—it shows you how even someone like Rembrandt didn't just spring full-blown but was in a tradition and just did more and went beyond the limits—"

I got so carried away with my topic that I did not immediately notice that Mr. Borges had moved quietly around to the front of his desk and was now practically sitting on my lap. As I looked up, he lunged.

I gave a semi-hysterical scream.

"You're the most wonderful person I've ever met!" he said. "A woman like you could understand me!"

"Mr. Borges," I cried, "you're on my *honors* committee!" I pushed him away and ran behind his desk. There was a determined gleam in his eye as he came toward me with his arms outstretched.

"Remember how awful my papers are!" I said.

"They're ten times better than the rest—but I feel you have so much more to give—that's why I've been hard on you."

This was like a scene out of *The Seventh Veil:* James Mason smacking the heroine's gifted hands with his cane. She would play only for him!

Mr. Borges pinned me against the wall, but I slithered out of his grip and circled the desk again.

"You—" I said, "you're—the Faculty Feeler!"

"These animals here would think up some crude term like that—"

I held my hands out to straight-arm him.

"Let's forget all about this," I said. "I'm sure you'll regret this in the morning."

"Laura—Laura—"

I grabbed for my purse, wishing I'd taken Freshman English. And Judo. As I grappled with the straps of my purse, he grabbed me and tried to wrestle me on to the desk—he managed a wet kiss on my cheek.

"Mr. Borges, come to your senses," I said. I hit him on

the head with my purse, which luckily contained a sculpture mallet, and stunned him enough to get out of the office. I raced down the dim hall as fast as I could go, without stopping to worry about muggers, escorts, darkness, or anything else.

I drove home in a daze.

My first conscious moment came when I found the garage empty. Bert wasn't home yet, thank God. I didn't want him to see me in this state. I raced to the bathroom, threw open the medicine chest, and searched for my bottle of tranquilizers. I'd need several. I tried to unscrew the lid, but it was a SAFE-T-KAP, childproof. I turned, thinking of how awful I'd felt in the assertiveness class, how backward I was. I pushed in, and turned, recalling Joe's maniacal eyes and the creepy byways of the campus. I rattled the bottle. How on earth did it open! Seeing Mr. Borges lunge and feeling the saliva from his kiss on my cheek. I put down the bottle. It didn't twist, push in, or have arrows that lined up. I grabbed a wet washcloth and bit into it to keep from screaming.

I was sitting there on the edge of the tub, chewing a cold washcloth and holding a tightly lidded bottle of pills in my hand, when Barney came creeping past in his black cape.

"For God's sake," I yelled, "have you been out running around the neighborhood in that outfit?"

"Yeah."

"Barney, what do you suppose the neighbors must think? They must be terrified. What would you feel if you saw someone dressed like that in the dark?"

I'd promised Bert to let Barney grow out of his phase naturally but I'd gone too far.

"And you might think of your father's reputation!" I screamed. "He's a *psychiatrist,* for God's sake! Have you got a screw loose?"

I sobbed into my washcloth.

"Gee, Mom," said Barney, "Dad never said anything."

"You know he doesn't believe in giving directions."

Barney looked at me with concern.

"Are you trying to get that bottle open?"

I looked down at the pills clenched tightly in my hand. Barney loosened my grip and pried the lid off the bottle.

"You just lift up," he said.

⚜ Chapter 27

"Bert, am I insured?" I asked.

"No."

"How much are *you* insured for?"

"Oh, about fifty–sixty thousand dollars. Don't worry, Laura, you'll be well provided for in the event of my death. I just worked out a new stock plan the other day."

"Why am I not insured?"

Bert looked up from his book.

"I never thought of it."

"I think I should be," I said. "And I should have money of my own. Do you know that I know practically nothing about our financial situation? All I do is take money out of our household box."

"I'll be glad to go over our books with you any time you want," he said. He gestured toward a stack of ledgers and boxes on his desk. "It'd bore you to tears, I'm sure."

"I think I should be better informed. We talked about money in the assertiveness class and I felt like an idiot."

Bert sighed at the mention of my group.

"You really don't have to do everything for yourself. I don't do everything for myself. I don't cook, clean—I'm helpless without you in the kitchen."

"I know."

"Okay—right after dinner I'll show you what we have."

After half an hour of listening to Bert describe savings plans, health insurance, and the state of our various mortgages, I was suppressing yawns that made my eyes water.

"Are you listening, Laura?" he said.

My attention had wandered to the shade of brown the couch was taking on as the sky darkened. With the fern behind it and the mauve of the wall and softening colors, the room beyond the desk light looked like a Vuillard painting. I tried to pretend to be brushing the hair out of my eyes as I made a miniature frame of my hands. If I could get those colors—

"This green book is our savings account, such as it is," lectured Bert. "But the thing is, if I were to die, you'd just go to Bill, my lawyer, and he'd straighten it all out for you."

"*Your* lawyer—that's what infuriates me," I suddenly blurted out. "Do you know that you say *my* lawyer, *my* house, *my* cabin—don't I share these things?"

Bert looked like Mr. Borges when I struck him on the head with my purse.

"Of course you do."

"Then why don't you say our lawyer, our house, our cabin?"

"It's just a word—a turn of phrase—"

"Just a word—and you a psychiatrist?"

"I'll try to stop saying it if it upsets you so."

"It does," I said. "I feel like a hired hand—or worse."

"No man could make money or have anything if his wife wasn't taking care of the children and the household—"

"Then it'd be *our* money."

"Such as it is."

"Then why is it all in your name? I really, I see, own nothing. I'm a pauper living in your house."

"You're not."

"Yes I am."

"Laura, it's great that you're going back to school, but if it's going to upset you—"

"Stop treating me like a fruit!" I said. "I think I should have some money of my own. If we really earned what we have together, then I should have control over some of it. I want a bank account of my own."

"No-no-no—that isn't necessary I tell you."

Bert was getting angry.

I retreated.

"You know you hate keeping books and bothering with money. And you're not the coolest math mind of the century . . ."

I fantasized selling a painting for more money than Bert made in a year.

"Laura, you're a good painter. You have beautiful taste in the house and you're a great cook when you put your mind to it—but a financial brain you're not. I'm providing very well. In fact, you'll be quite well off in the event of my death."

It couldn't be too soon to suit me.

☗ Chapter 28

Maybe it was the end-of-the-quarter blues, but I felt pretty low as I shopped for a piece of stone to carve my figure in. Or maybe it was the dull cold knowledge that the art history paper I'd worked so hard on was in the hands of a man who'd tried to seduce me and whom I had beaned with a sculpture mallet.

I hadn't seen Judy since Christmas. If I stopped in to see her, I thought, her misery might cheer me up. Things could be worse, after all: I could be in her situation.

One afternoon on the way home from school, I rang Judy's doorbell. Her fourteen-year-old daughter, Millicent, answered.

"Oh, hi, Laura—c'mon in."

"Is your mother at home?"

"She's at the beauty shop," said Millicent. "Should be back any minute. Want to sit down?"

I took a seat at the kitchen table.

"Coffee?"

"Thanks."

"Gee, Laura," said Millicent, "you look beat."

"Yeah," I said. "How's your mom?"

"Great. She and Daddy are divorcing, you know."

"I know."

"Terry's living here with us," said Millicent. "He and

Mom will probably get married when the decree is final, but I don't know why they don't just keep the arrangement as is. Less hassle."

With this, Terry, a six-foot Adonis, about twenty-nine years old, wearing a tight tee-shirt and jeans, pushed open the kitchen door.

"Millicent, I'm leaving for class—where's my salt-rising dough?"

"I moved it to the counter."

"Oh."

Terry lifted a large crockery bowl that contained what looked like a human abdomen covered with a napkin. He shook hands over the top of the breathing mass.

"Hi."

"Are you still teaching the gourmet cooking class?" I asked.

"Yes, we're doing breads, as you might gather," said Terry. "I start teaching the ladies simple techniques: kneading, rolling, how to handle dough."

It sounded so sensual, especially accompanied by Terry's gestures. He patted the abdomen-like dough fondly.

"Then we go on to spicier things: herbs, cheeses—we jazz the basics up a bit."

He opened the door and started out.

"Oh, Millicent—put the loaf of bread I made for dinner into the oven and tell Judy I'll be home in plenty of time to finish the casserole and make a salad. So long. Nice meeting you, Laura."

He was the handsomest young man I'd ever seen.

" 'Scuse me a minute," said Millicent. She took a pan from the counter and put it in the oven. By the time we heard Judy's car pull into the drive, the kitchen smelled of fresh bread. I could see in the dining room a table set with wine glasses and cut flowers.

"Daddy's coming over for dinner," said Millicent.

"Terry and I are going all-out to make him feel comfortable. I mean, we don't want him to feel replaced or —you know what I mean?"

I nodded.

"Of course."

"Laura!"

Judy burst into the kitchen and threw her arms around me.

"Where have you *been?*"

"Just busy—the grind."

"You looked peaked."

Judy, on the other hand, looked radiant. She had lost about twenty pounds, had acquired instant chic, and her hair looked terrific in a short, blown-dry, casual cut. She poured herself some coffee, refilled my cup, and sat down.

"So tell me what's new," she said. "Are you getting your degree in the spring?"

"If I don't flunk Art History," I said.

Millicent tactfully excused herself, and Judy was soon telling me all about her new lifestyle.

"At first I was crushed," she said. "Just crushed. I'd be all alone. I couldn't manage. I felt rejected, blah, blah, blah. But things have worked out very well."

I sniffed the fresh bread.

"Steve was angry at first, but I got him to go to a shrink and he realized I wasn't rejecting him; it was a growth thing. A matter of experiencing our existential possibilities. He's been very generous. When we were married, he was so Victorian—doled out every cent—but he's promised faithfully to pay for Millicent's education and has agreed to a very fair settlement. When Terry and I get married I'm going to keep my own name and my own money."

And Terry can cook, I thought.

"Now how about you? Is Bert accepting your new role or is he being Bertish?"

"He's being somewhat Bertish," I said. "Actually, things are not too bad, but I'm tired. We need a holiday—just the two of us. I keep wishing he'd take me off with him for a weekend. All those sick people at Christmas, and school—the puppies—the children—we never have any time for ourselves—"

"Why don't you take *him* off for a weekend?"

"Me?"

"Sure. Why should he take you?"

"You don't understand. I couldn't make a decision like that. The money—"

"Don't you have any money?"

"No—"

"Well, plan the weekend anyway. Bert would probably enjoy it."

"You don't know Bert, Judy. He's really a very old-fashioned man. He likes to be the knight in armor who protects the lady in the tower."

"Bert's a doll," said Judy. "You're lucky."

Judy's face clouded just slightly—the only indication she gave of not being completely in control.

☗ Chapter 29

"What are you doing at spring break?" I asked Sister Margaret.

"Going to Montana for a job interview and then I celebrate Easter with my folks."

She was washing clay off her hands in the big studio sink.

"A high school?"

"Right. I'd be teaching art five periods a day."

"Wow."

"I'm stayin' home with my kids," said Tony. "What are you and Bert doing?"

"I'm not sure," I said. I realized we'd be without the usual family gathering and felt lonely. Poppa was not going out of the house, and Gail had written that she was heading for Fort Lauderdale with the college kids. Mother was staying put to play in a tournament with her bridge club.

I pushed the stone that I'd hauled into the studio against a wall, and looked at the plaster lady I was going to copy in it next quarter. I felt smug. Ron would never learn carving from Mr. Rubel. The twin monsters had no shape whatsoever; Mr. Rubel had simply chipped away an inch or two and given them a textured surface.

"They can't be tombstones," I said to Sister.

"He *is* an undertaker."

"I know, but he directs funerals; he doesn't bury people."

"Hi, folks."

It was Bob. He was dressed in a neat gabardine suit and he had gotten a haircut. There was something determined about his bearing.

"I'm going straight," he said.

"What do you mean?"

"Getting an honest job. I won't be back next quarter."

We all crowded around him.

"But you're so *good*."

"What're you going to do?"

"Join the Peace Corps." He sat down on a stool. "Between the high cost of going to school and what I hear about the job market, I thought I'd better make this move," he said. "I can't live by selling paintings, and every teaching job has a couple of hundred applicants."

"That's what I'm afraid of," said Sister. "And I have to pay my own way to Montana to find out."

We sat grouped around the clay-covered pedestals and shared the gloom. Only Mr. Rubel looked happy. He always had work.

While Bob told us about his training program, he never once looked directly at Dora.

Ms. Saffron, who had never visited the sculpture studio before, suddenly appeared and went from one student's work to another, studying the forms. She stopped in front of mine and looked from the white plaster cast to my untouched, formless stone.

"You're not going to carve that woman in stone, are you?" she demanded.

"That was the general idea," I said.

She looked at the figure again. I had been proud of the fact that my sculpture was natural and balanced: I had not resorted to an exaggerated pose or outlandish proportions to gain interest. Ms. Saffron was frowning.

"You don't like it?" I asked.

"It's so goddamned *dull!*" she said. She grabbed a handful of soft clay and, rolling it between her fingers, stuck what resembled an arm on the figure's back.

"Women need more than two arms, Laura; you of all people ought to know that," she said. She stuck another "arm" on each side of the cast just below the breasts, and another pair below those. I was so furious at her attack on my work, I could not respond at first. A modest white figure with multiple gray arms, my figure resembled an Indian deity.

"There—now at least it's interesting!" said Ms. Saffron.

I stared at the bizarre transformed lady before me.

I liked her.

Instead of blowing up at Ms. Saffron, according to my first impulse, I said, "I'll keep the extra arms, but I'm going to model them—give them some structure."

"Great," said Ms. Saffron.

Bob, Sister, and the others stood by, staring in awe.

"These have to be placed so I can carve them without chipping them off," I said.

I removed the stuck-on appendages and proceeded to replace them with forms that matched the rest of the figure.

The scene between me and Ms. Saffron had a strange effect on the group: we went wild.

"What're we going to give Bob for a send-off?" asked Sister Margaret.

"A party!" cried Tony Ramira.

Bob's eyes lit up happily.

"My place," he said. "I'll even splurge on some wine!"

"We'll all bring a bottle!" said Sister.

"I'll treat," insisted Mr. Rubel.

"I'm in," said Ms. Saffron.

The group began to pack up chisels, mallets, and drawing boards, and moved toward the door almost as a unit. Only Dora, Mrs. Goldfarb, and I hung back.

"I've got to get Henry's dinner," said Mrs. Goldfarb. "Best of luck in your new career, Bob."

Bob gave her a little peck on the cheek and looked at the other two hold-outs.

"I'm sorry," said Dora, "I have to pass. I've got a date."

"I'd better scoot on home, too," I said. "I—"

"Oh, c'mon, Laura, one drink—" said Ms. Saffron.

"It wouldn't be the same without you," said Bob.

"Yeah," chimed in Ron.

They really seemed to want me—and of course Sister Margaret would not want to go alone. Though she appeared to be one of the ring leaders.

"No—I'd better go home—" I said. The others had packed up, and I too reached for my purse and car keys.

"What shall I get—red or white?" shouted Mr. Rubel. The group was getting noisy, as if already high on wine.

"Little of each," said Ms. Saffron.

"What do you say, Laura?"

Oh, what the hell, I thought. Bert was going to be at a dinner meeting, Barney and Donald could fix their own dinner. I didn't want to get an old lady's peck on the cheek from Bob.

"Right with you," I said. "I'm going to call home and tell the kids to go ahead with dinner."

The others cheered.

"We better stop for something to eat too," said Sister. "Wine on an empty stomach—"

"I'll get some cold cuts," said Tony, "as my contribution. That's my new independence. I don't cook. Does everybody like salami and cheese?"

A cheer went up for Tony, and the group, me a part of

it, moved down the hall noisily, picking up celebrants as we passed the various studio doors. Those of us who drove packed our cars with riders: I had Mr. Sanders with Tony on his lap, Ron, Sister Margaret, and assorted friends of Bob's.

"One more week!" someone shouted.

"Then free at last. Thank God Almighty, free at last!"

"I'm going to ask Mr. Rubel tonight what those things are," vowed Sister Margaret.

"Not when he's buying the wine," said Ron. It was the first sensible comment he'd ever made.

Sister Margaret began to cackle hysterically.

"The picture of Ms. Saffron putting those extra arms on your figure was the funniest thing I've ever seen!" she said.

"I thought Laura was going to smack her," said Tony. "But Mrs. Cool just took it quietly and went right back to work."

"Mrs. Cool?" I asked.

"You're unflappable!" said Ron.

This from Nirvana City. I began to blush.

"I'm *not* unflappable," I said.

"Yes you are," said Sister. "I've been at your house."

Why did I feel I had to defend myself? I must seem like a real square, a prude, a bourgeoise.

Maybe that's why I practically dived into the wine bottle when we got to Bob's. Mr. Rubel arrived just as we did and before we even looked around and sat down we were knocking back jelly glasses of chablis. Only Ron passed.

"I never touch alcohol," he said; he assumed his guru position in the middle of Bob's tiny living room.

"I'll just have a joint."

Ron rolled his cigarette and passed it around to those who wanted a puff.

"Très wicked, eh?" asked Sister Margaret. She was next

to me on the couch as it came my way. I thought of all those lectures I'd given Barney and friends on marijuana and the drug scene. I took a quick puff. And all those on resisting peer pressure. I passed the joint to Mr. Sanders.

"Thank you, Mrs. Hoffman," said he. He had loosened his striped, old-school tie, and was lurching on the edge of the couch like one of Ron's soft sculptures. After a puff of the cigarette, he stood up and began an arcane lecture on the art of perspective. Bob seized him like a dancing partner and whirled him around the room.

"If the vortex doesn't get you, the matrix will!" Bob sang.

We all joined in.

"A new musical!" shouted one of the younger men. *"Paint Your Canvasses!"*

"The story of an art department in a small midwestern college beset by budget crunch and governmental regulations!"

"The student body includes an undertaker," someone said.

Mr. Rubel beamed. He had stood throughout the party, inscrutable as his work.

"Heavy symbolism."

"And an incompetent dean named Pointless!"

Everything we said or shouted seemed terrifically witty when washed down by chablis and valpolicella. We lost track of the time completely. It was only five o'clock in the afternoon. I caught sight of my face in a mirror—flushed and singing louder than anyone else.

Pretty soon Sister and I were clutching a gooseneck lamp for a microphone and doing the Andrews Sisters' routines from the forties. Mr. Sanders was held up by the two of us—a reluctant third sister. He was too young to know the words. We were brought back for several encores.

When we collapsed on the couch from our efforts, Ms. Saffron said, "I didn't think you were old enough to know those songs, Laura."

"I'm not," I said.

"She was a child bride," said Sister, "married at twelve."

"And how in the hell," I said, "did I get to be everybody's fall guy? I got blamed for my mother's problems and now I get blamed for my children's—I get so tired of being a responsible pershon—"

"That's responshible perthon," said Bob.

"Food time," called Tony.

She coaxed us to the table in Bob's tiny, crowded kitchen and waved at a tray of salami, cheese, and bread.

"Why do I feel guilty for not cooking a feast for this crowd?" Tony said. "I didn't even know we were going to have a party."

"This is *beautiful*, Tony," said I. "Just beautiful."

The reds and yellows of the tray of food began to spin around madly and that's the last thing I remember about Bob's farewell party.

The sky was dark when I opened my eyes again, and through the gloom I saw an unfamiliar crack running down the bedroom wall from ceiling to floor. Next to the crack was one of Bob's paintings. Strange. My eye traveled to the bed: an Indian print throw was crumpled at the foot of it. I didn't own such a cover. My eye, now horrified, traveled farther and I saw my right leg wrapped around both of Bob's. I turned my face and stared into his open eyes.

"Oh God," I said.

I was relieved to see that we were both dressed.

All I could utter was a little clicking sound in my throat.

My head was on Bob's shoulder and an arm flung across his chest.

"What happened?" I said. I tried to move away.

"No, don't move," said Bob. "And don't worry. You were in no condition to do anything but sleep, believe me."

"I think I've got a virus," I said.

He laughed uproariously.

"A virus?" he shouted.

"I feel weak and my head hurts."

"You were a little—uh—intoxicated, shall we say?"

"Me?"

"Yes—don't you remember? You were doing the Andrews Sisters and then when Tony served the food you passed out."

It was all being replayed in my mind: the gooseneck lamp, what I'd said—what everyone else had said. I vaguely remembered people calling good-bye as I lay on Bob's bed in a cold sweat.

"After the party you raved a little more about what a responshible pershon you are and then you threw up in the toilet and then you fell asleep again. I guess I did too. I wasn't in real great shape myself. And here we are."

I untangled myself from Bob, gradually regaining a little strength. He pulled me back to him gently.

"We've had this date for a long time, sister." His Marlon Brando was not too bad—certainly as good as my Patty Andrews.

Why not? I thought. I was determined to experience my times—this was part of them. Also, I'd already made a complete ass of myself: things couldn't get much worse. I relaxed.

"Did you take a puff on that joint Ron was passing around?" asked Bob. He was nibbling my ear.

"Just a tiny one," I said.

"I thought maybe you did and weren't used to it. How in hell much wine did you drink?"

"Who're you?" I demanded, "Senator McCarthy?"

"Why not?" said Bob.

"Such a son of a bitch."

Bob halted in mid-caress and looked me in the eye.

"McCarthy a son of a bitch?" he said.

"Absolutely. The worst. A real rat."

Bob sat up.

"I can't believe what I'm hearing, Laura. If it hadn't been for Gene McCarthy we'd still be in Vietnam."

I felt as though a cold hose had been turned on me. I sat up.

"I meant *the* Senator McCarthy—Joe," I said. I hopped off the bed and sat in the one chair in the room, an old sofa pillow. I couldn't have made love with Bob if I were paid to—in spite of his firm young torso peeking out of his unbuttoned shirt.

"Bob, I'm sorry—I realize I've led you on in the worst way—" I patted my disheveled hair and clothes pointlessly.

"What's wrong?" he asked.

"It's just—I suddenly remembered I have a husband—whom I love." And who would *know* I meant Joe McCarthy, I thought. How could I have a fling with a guy who was sucking on a pacifier during the Army–McCarthy hearings?

"You're not mad over a political disagreement?" said Bob.

"No—no," I said. "I really do love my husband and we've always trusted one another. What time is it?" I held my watch up to my ear. It had stopped at six o'clock.

Bob rolled over and picked up his watch from the bedside table.

"Quarter of eleven."

"If I leave now I'll get home in time to let Bert open the garage door for me—"

Bob looked so confused and hurt that I felt I must take a few more minutes to comfort him. He reminded me of Donald when he'd flunked spelling.

"It's nothing to do with you, Bob. You're the nicest, sexiest, best-looking man I've ever met." I leaned over and kissed him on the cheek. I was Deborah Kerr in *Tea and Sympathy*—but Bob wouldn't know about that, either. "What would Donald think of the two of us if he could see us now?" I asked.

Bob sighed and looked resigned. He ran his hands through his hair.

"You want some coffee?" he said. "It's instant."

"No—but I'll borrow a shot of Listerine," I said. "I don't think my breath is springtime fresh."

As Bob went to the bathroom to get the mouthwash, I gathered together my raincoat and purse.

He served us each a tumblerful of Listerine.

"Here's looking at you, kid," said he.

As we sat on his bed gargling, I had a painful, terrible, terminal attack of remorse.

I'd missed all the fun. I wasn't an insatiably sexy free spirit like the liberated heroines I'd been reading about. I'd embarrassed a real friend, competed with Judy, deceived Bert.

I did not, I decided, approve of adultery. At least it was not my bag. I wanted to be home with a mature man. I was too old to be a Bohemian. Bob was too young for me—and besides, his apartment was depressingly seedy.

"Bob," I said, "I don't suppose you can ever forgive me for acting like such a loony!" I burst into tears. "I've made such a dreadful fool out of myself!"

Bob patted my shoulder.

"You're just human, Laura."

"Who me?" I said. "Nonsense!" I wiped my tears, stood up, and threw my raincoat around my shoulders. "I'm Super-Mom! Cézanne and Betty Crocker all rolled into one. A devil in the bedroom and the Angel in the House." I strode to the door, my raincoat-cape flying behind me.

Bob lay back on his bed and shook his head. As I closed the door, he still looked puzzled, but he gave me the peace sign.

When I got home, Bert was already in bed. I took a shower, gargled again, and crawled in beside him. He put his arms around me and wrapped his legs around mine.

"I've been at a meeting," said I.

"Umm."

"Well, more like a party," I added. "At Bob's."

"Umm."

"Aren't you going to ask me what we did?"

"Do I look like the Un-American Activities Committee?" Bert mumbled. It was good to be home.

"I thought you might be insanely jealous."

Bert gave me a sleepy but passionate kiss.

"I trust you," he said.

"How was *your* meeting?" I asked.

"Okay."

"Who was there?"

"Dr. Howard, Dr. Stern, Bill Berman—whole bunch."

I could have sworn Bert had had a drink or two.

"Were there any women?"

"A few."

"What do you do at your meetings?"

"For heaven's sake, Laura, I'm about to pass out," said Bert. "What do you think we do?"

I'd never given it a second thought—before.

"Bert, I trust you, too," I said.

He didn't hear me; he was asleep.

I looked about at my familiar surroundings. At Bert's head on the pillow. I really did love Bert—and had all the sex I could handle. If only more often we could find times and places away from our responsibilities.

The next day, I was back at work on my plaster woman. I stared into her blank white eyes.

"A woman needs eight arms," I lectured her, "not eight heads."

When I got home from school, I called a state park and made reservations for Bert and me for Friday and Saturday of the holiday. We'd have several days to ourselves and be home in time for Easter.

Chapter 30

Bert went along willingly with my plan for a retreat.

"I'll have to cancel a meeting," he said, "but we don't get much done on Good Friday anyway." It wasn't the most romantic of responses, but at least he accepted my taking the lead.

Now I had only to deliver Fluffy to the vet for her surgery, and to settle the matter of a sitter. You don't casually leave a house and a young boy in charge of someone who'd been behaving as Barney had all year. On the other hand, Donald seemed a little mature for sitters. He habitually answered the phone when we called from someplace away from home and reported on the sitter's comfort and well-being. Further, Barney had suddenly transformed himself into an ultraconservative. He had taken to wearing a jacket, a white shirt, and even a tie. His new ambition was to be an insurance actuary.

"Well," I said, "do you boys think you can take care of each other for a couple of days while Dad and I have a holiday?"

"Sure," said Donald. "But why would you and Dad want to go someplace without us? What will you do?"

"Oh, we'll think of something," I said. "We'll miss you, though. Be careful to turn off the stove. Lock the doors."

"Be cool, Mom," said Barney. "Really, we're better off without those nutty sitters you used to get for us. One of them was psycho. Always creeping up behind you like Joan Crawford in *Straitjacket*."

In spite of all the protestations about how well they would do without us, both Barney and Donald developed symptoms before we left. Barney got athlete's foot and Donald claimed his freckles had become swollen.

"Come here and let me see," I said. I was packing shorts and slacks into a suitcase. Donald sat on the edge of my bed and presented his bare back and neck. His freckles *were* swollen. Or was I anxious too?

By the time Bert and I pulled out of the driveway, Donald's freckles had flattened out. He was engaged in a game of foursquare and barely turned around to wave good-bye.

Quailridge State Park provided swimming, hiking, biking, tennis, shuffleboard, boating, and badminton. Bert and I sat in the sun and watched the other lodge guests enjoying these pursuits. We were too tired to move. When we wearied of the activity-watching we turned our attention to the patterns of the leaves and listened to the hum of motorboats on the lake. Our cottage had a screened porch over the water and we pulled our bed out there at night to enjoy the breeze and the moonlight. I wanted to tell Bert about the fiasco with Bob but hesitated; I didn't want to spoil our idyll. I'd tell him in about six months, when Bob was safely at work in Pakistan.

Things were going beautifully until on Saturday evening at dinner Bert began one of his harangues on our finances. These came out of the blue regularly, but this time his concern for me seemed to hark back to my request for more direct participation and control. Referring to some insurance plan, he hinted at how well off I'd be when he died and said, "Of course, the best way to go is by accident while engaging in business. Then you can get the benefit of double-indemnity."

"Really, Bert," I said. "This is hardly romantic."

He ignored me. He was deep into the complications of stock options and estate taxes.

"Now, Laura," he said, barely looking up from his dinner, "would you like me to arrange for you to have full control of everything when I die, so you can have immediately usable funds, or put some in trust at a higher interest rate?"

"I better have the ready cash," I said. "I may need to get myself a gigolo."

At last he looked up.

"Bert, *will* you stop talking about your death? Does my wanting some control over my own life make you think you're being killed off?"

He frowned.

"I was just—"

"Just *what?* I asked you to settle some money on me now—I'm not planning to be a widow—I don't even want to think about it. I'm interested in life and in now."

"But I don't see the importance—"

"You're keeping a measure of *control* over me."

He ran his hands through his hair.

"I can't figure out what you *want,*" he said. "First you said you just wanted to go back to school—and now—"

"Give them an inch and they'll take a mile," I said.

It was the end of a beautiful weekend.

On the way home, I said, "Shall we stop at the supermarket and get Easter baskets?"

Bert brightened up. Holiday rituals always put him in a good mood. We bought green paper grass, baskets, chocolate bunnies, blue and purple eggs, and jelly beans. In the car I arranged a basket for Donald and one for our sixteen-year-old in the gray flannel suit.

"I wish Gail were going to be home," said Bert.

"So do I."

"Do you suppose Roy is with her in Florida?"

"Probably."

"I just never could figure out how serious they are. I think Gail's so young . . ."

"I know."

When we got home, Donald and Barney were peacefully asleep. The house didn't look much the worse for their care. While Bert slipped the Easter baskets under their beds, I went through the mail. A bright postcard picturing white sand, blue ocean, and palm trees caught my attention. I stared at the scene for a full moment, afraid to turn it over and read the message.

A moment later, I went running after Bert.

"Guess what? Guess what?"

"What is it?" said Bert.

"They're getting married!"

He took the postcard out of my hand.

"Roy and Gail?" he asked.

"No," I said, "Mother and Dr. Brach!"

Chapter 31

As I faced the final quarter at school, Fluffy was running around with her hindquarters on wheels and had to be carried up and down the steps. She was playing the role of invalid to the hilt. Mother announced her intention to be married in Cincinnati with full fanfare, and I'd have to put on a wedding.

"Couldn't you just say no?" said Bert.

"My mother didn't speak to me for two years because I once forgot Mother's Day," I said.

"At least she picked a good man."

I read aloud from the letter that had followed Mother's surprising postcard:

> We both like bridge and Herbert says he will retire in a year or two so I don't have to sell my home here. We'd like to get married in May and have the ceremony and reception at your house, where we met. Did you get the drapes up in the den?

Bert sighed.

"I don't see how you're going to give a big wedding when you're in school all day."

I folded up the letter and tucked it in a desk drawer. Such happy news! But I just couldn't deal with giving a wedding at the moment.

A foul-up in the University computer and the fact that

Mr. Borges was reported to be "sick" had kept us from getting our grades, even on last quarter's final paper. I could very well be failing Art History. Suppose I'd given Mr. Borges a concussion?

"What's wrong with him?" I had asked Sister.

"No one knows."

Maybe I should drop a few courses, I thought, and graduate next year. Donald firmed up my plans.

"Are you going to graduate in June?" he asked.

"I don't know," I said. "I had hoped so. Why do you ask?"

"I've been telling my friends that my mom is working on a college degree and they keep asking when you're going to graduate."

"Well—I hope to finish this quarter. But I can't be sure: if I flunk Art History I'll owe them a credit, and Grandma's getting married. Just tell them I might graduate, but if I don't—say I had to take some extra work."

"I think I better just tell them my mom died," he said.

The morning of registration, the roofers and painters, who had given me estimates in fall, arrived with ladders, buckets, and trucks full of tools. I would have sent them away, but workmen were too difficult to get, and with Mother getting married, the house would have to be in good shape.

"Going to be peaceful working here," I said to Bert.

"Don't forget to tell them to fix that light over the kitchen door while they're here and show them the leak in the basement window."

As I talked to the foreman, all the good sections at school in painting and sculpture were filling up. I'd get Ms. Saffron and Ron again.

But at least I'd learned *something* from Kim in assertiveness training. No more would I be the Laura who

172

listened to the roofer's vertigo problems and placed the highest tiles for him. When the construction foreman arrived, I established at the outset that *I* was the sick one.

Limping badly, I went to greet Mr. Williams, who would be supervising the various crews.

"My husband and I both have bad backs," I said. "We can stand very little strain."

He clutched at his heart. He'd been in the construction business a long time.

"Sorry," I said, "but I've got a heart murmur too and migraine headaches. You must get this work done on schedule."

Looking harassed at my definite stand, Mr. Williams wiped his eyes.

"I'll try," he said, "but my doctor says I might be developing cataracts."

"Could you possibly help me into the house?" I said. "I think one of my dizzy spells is coming on."

It was afternoon before I could get to the University. The lines would be interminable, but I solved that problem by borrowing a three-year-old boy from a neighbor. With him along, I was pushed to the head of the lines.

To dispatch the forms in a reasonable time, I killed off both parents and saved having to list their childhood diseases.

At the vet's I produced Barney and his electric guitar, which I assured the receptionist was warping badly every moment it sat in the humid car. I was getting as crooked as Crawley—who was selling the art supplies he got free on financial aid.

"Unorthodox," said Bert, when I told him of my new methods, "but I suppose it represents growth."

When classes resumed, I chipped away at my stone woman, carefully blocking out each of her eight arms. I thought more and more of what I wanted to do with my degree—if I got it. I did not want to return to the basement. I would have to get a job—but doing what?

"I should have taken law or public accounting," I told Bert.

"God save us from you as a CPA," he said. "As a lawyer, you'd do fine."

"A Fine Arts degree in painting, sculpture, and drawing doesn't lead one right into a job," I said.

"Laura, you don't need a job," said Bert.

"Yes, I do." I continued to mull over the opportunities. Not only did I not have a real vocation for teaching but there were no openings. I'd have to try some advertising agencies, but my work did not seem to have much commercial potential. Would I have to meet deadlines? Draw what they told me? I'd been doing just what I wanted to all these years. Maybe I could sell to galleries. But I was still too shy to take my work around.

I got all *A*'s on my report card, which the computer finally spit out. The ones from Ron and Borges didn't count too much; Ron was a nut case and Borges perhaps afraid of blackmail. But the other two boosted my self-esteem. Almost high enough to face the job market.

"Sister Margaret's got a job teaching in Montana," I told Bert, "and Bob's going into the Peace Corps."

"Did you ask the dean about part-time teaching?"

"No openings," I said. "And stacks of letters from better-qualified people with higher degrees waiting to get whatever comes up."

"I don't suppose you'd be satisfied to work on your own—"

"Not after all this effort. Besides, I want independence. And I want to contribute financially to the family. You know what Simone de Beauvoir says—"

"Spare me," said Bert.

"Sister Margaret is really doing something. She's going to a little town way up in the Montana mountains. She'll be teaching all these kids, and she's good—she'll have them loving art. She's going to buy a lot and build her own cabin!"

"But, Laura," said Bert, "she's a nun."

"Do you have to be a *nun* to do something?"

"It helps," said Bert. "You have children and a home."

"So do you."

"You already have a cabin."

"And I love it," I said. "But I'd like to see the world."

"Today art school—tomorrow ze vorld!" said Bert.

"While we're on the subject of my working"—I took a deep breath. Kim said I had to do this—"I can't believe you can't make a sandwich for yourself."

Bert looked stricken.

"I come from an old-fashioned home. I was never allowed in the kitchen."

"You'll have to learn to make your own lunch if you insist on coming home instead of eating in the cafeteria like all the other husbands."

I took bread and baloney from the refrigerator.

"You see," I said, "you take a piece of bread"—plop!— "you spread mayonnaise on it"—slosh!—"you put a slice of baloney on it"—plop!—"and another slice of bread. Result? Sandwich."

"It looks simple enough," said Bert. "I guess I can do it." This from a man who could take the entire human brain apart and put it back together.

"It's you I'll miss," he said.

A day or two later, I got my hair cut and one of the new frizzy permanents. I threw my blow dryer and curling iron away.

"How do you like it?" I asked Bert.

"It looks nice," he said, "but then it always did."

"This is ten times easier. All I do is dry it with a towel and push it around a little."

"You've confronted Mr. Williams, the builder, you've confronted the system at City U., you've confronted me, and you've even confronted your hairdresser," said Bert. "Don't you think it's time to stand up to your mother?"

"How?" I said. "I can't tell her to take her business elsewhere."

"No, but she can postpone the wedding until June—it's a more traditional month for brides than May anyway, and by then you'll be out of school."

I started to defend, but bit my tongue.

"You're right," I said. "I'm too old to be afraid of my mother. Would you tell her, Bert?"

He made a strange clicking sound in his throat.

"Just kidding—just kidding."

When I called and told Mother we'd have to postpone, she said, "Oh."

I could just see her lips drawing into a tight, hurt line.

"We'll have a lovely ceremony, just as soon as school is out."

"I see."

"It will be much better. I'll have time to concentrate. I'm so rushed now."

"I understand."

"You do?"

"Herbert and I could get married at his club," she said.

I had to beg her to have the wedding at our house.

But we set the date for June.

Chapter 32

"Anybody want to go out to Creative Systems, Inc.? There's a job opening for an artist," said Mr. Sanders. "You have to be a good draftsman."

"That lets me out," said Tony, "and anyway I got another year to go. You try it, Laura."

Yesterday I would have said no. But the new me refused to be frightened.

"What is Creative Systems, Inc.?" I asked.

"Some kind of media lab, it says here." He read from a card. "Total environment education using creative, innovative media techniques."

I took the card. It wouldn't hurt to try.

"I suppose I have to take along a résumé," I said to Sister.

"Haven't you ever gone on a job interview before?" she asked.

"Not really."

I was embarrassed to be so much more cloistered than a nun.

"What do you put on a résumé?" I said.

"Vital statistics, and then just list all the things you've done professionally—the ones that pertain to the job."

I wrote my name—Laura Williams Hoffman—it took up

more space that way. I added my other vital statistics to what suddenly seemed like a huge piece of typing paper. Then I was stumped. I hadn't done anything professionally except paint a lot in my basement.

"It's pretty blank," I said to Sister.

"Well then, list all the shows you've been in, the boards you've served on, civic work, stuff like that."

"May I see how you did yours?" I asked.

At the lunch break, Sister and I went to her locker where she produced a three-page document.

"List your degrees and educational background and publications," she said.

"You haven't named anything yet that I can list."

I read Sister's Vitae: University of Chicago, B.A., Liberal Arts, B.S. Teachers' College, major in art; 15 years teaching, St. Mary's High School; in-service courses, Skidmore; M.A., City University, Cincinnati (June) ; co-editor *Secondary Arts Curriculum;* President, Art Teachers' Association; Parish President, Community Reach Program in Urban Arts—and so on.

"Thanks," I said.

I went back to my blank paper.

"I think one page is probably more impressive than too many—don't you, Bert?"

"Could be."

"That way they might think I'm so great I just couldn't list everything and decided to be selective . . ."

I wrote my name and address, birthdate, phone number, and the names and current activities of my husband and children. I didn't want the interviewer to think I hadn't been doing anything all these years. I added:

DEGREE: Bachelor of Fine Arts, City University (official in June, I hope)

COURSES: Painting, Drawing, Sculpture, Art History
ORGANIZATIONS: PTA, Unitarian Church, Great Books
CIVIC WORK: Muscular Dystrophy, block chairman;
    Brownies, paper drive

With a lot of impressive white space to set off the type, it made a page.

The Creative Systems, Inc., building was in a suburban business center. It looked like a large space capsule that had just arrived on its green launching pad. There were no windows. I walked up the steps and went through the futuristic glass doors.

"Mr. Milhard, please," I said to the secretary. "I have an appointment."

"Mil-*lard*," said she. "Please have a seat. I'll let him know you're here."

I sat down on a Mies vander Rohe chair and thumbed through a magazine. I was too nervous to even look at the pictures. After twenty minutes of waiting, I called to the secretary, "Uh—excuse me, is there a ladies' room?"

"Through there," she said, indicating a doorway.

"If Mr. Mil-hard—"

"Mil-*lard*," she said.

"If Mr. Mil-*lard* comes out before I—just tell him—I'll be back soon."

I gestured ineffectually.

She nodded and looked as though she had eaten a bad piece of liverwurst.

I needn't have worried about making Mr. Whatever-His-Name-Was wait; when I returned, the sitting room was still quiet and the secretary did not look up. I checked the card I'd been given; there was definitely an "h" in the man's name. After another half hour of thumbing through magazines and wondering if I'd have to go back to the ladies' room, a loud buzzer sounded and the secretary gestured to me to go into the inner office.

"Mr. *Mil*-hard," I said, trying to sound hearty and unafraid.

He shook my hand.

"Mil-*lard*," said he. He was a huge, athletic-looking man with snow-white hair and a deep tan. "Won't you sit down, Mrs. Hoffman?"

I sat, completely dwarfed by him and his enormous desk, which he sat behind like the Wizard of Oz. I wasn't sure the room wasn't tilted.

"Now why do you want to come to work for me, Mrs. Hoffman?" he asked.

"Well, I don't know," I said. "I'm not just sure what Creative Systems, Inc., is; I was hoping you'd elucidate a bit. The ad at the art school—"

He held out a hand. Not to worry. He understood. No lengthy explanations, please.

Why did his every gesture seem like one up for him and a demerit for me?

"I am a producer of educational systems," he said. "I have worked with educational institutions all over the globe. I just flew in this morning, for instance, from Hawaii where I was doing a presentation on their agricultural situation. My pilot prefers the shorter treks so he can see his wife and children, but since he gets thirty thousand a year, he doesn't complain too loudly."

I was thoroughly impressed. But not enlightened.

"What would these 'presentations' consist of? I was told you needed a good draftsman. Oh—my résumé," I said. I smacked my forehead. "And I brought a portfolio in case you wanted to see some of my drawings."

He reached out for the résumé and looked it over.

"Very impressive," he said.

Now I knew he was strange.

"I still don't understand exactly what I'd be doing," I said. "Would I—or whoever you hire"—I added modestly —"be doing sketches for these presentations?"

"We go in for visual media but sometimes sketches are part of the creative process."

"But what exactly are Creative Systems?"

"We originate, distribute, and show films on educational topics."

Oh I hope I'm not in a porn studio, I thought. Mr. Milhard was so evasive.

"I've really no training in films," I said.

"Let me see your drawings."

I untied the string of my portfolio, and he quickly glanced through my drawings.

"Could you do cartoon-type things?" he asked. "You seem to have a fairly bold line."

"I might," I said.

"Technical subjects sometimes need a light touch. We did a nifty film on the manufacture of rugs, and the creative resource person helped us get the explanatory part across with a kangaroo who kept pulling a pointer and blackboard out of her pouch. You have to catch the audience's interest."

"What kind of audiences do you have?"

"Schoolchildren—almost exclusively."

The work didn't sound impossible. I thought I'd better get businesslike if I wanted to be considered.

"What does the job pay?" I asked.

"A good artist can make twenty to twenty-five thousand dollars to start," he said. "There's really no limit, depending on your creativity and ability to put across your ideas. You have to give me concepts for presentation of material that I can sell to the big companies."

"How do the big companies get in here? Aren't these educational films?"

"Yes, but they have to be financed. We just had a pineapple company, for example, sponsor our film on Hawaii. The children learn about the Fiftieth State."

"What do the companies get out of it?"

"The children also learn fiscal awareness."

"You mean the films *ad*vertise—in *schools?*" I shrieked.

"Consumer Philosophy is a necessary part of everyone's education, Mrs. Hoffman."

"And the artist only gets paid if and when one of these ideas sells, is that it—I mean there's no—fiscal regularity?"

"After you start moving projects, there would be—we have a man on the coast who draws fifty thousand dollars like clockwork."

My expression must have given away my distaste for Mr. Milhard's business.

"Mrs. Hoffman, it was good of you to come in and chat with us," he said. "But I have the feeling that you're not sufficiently interested in this kind of work."

"If you mean I'm against advertising commercial products under the guise of educational movies, you're correct," I said.

"As I thought," returned Mr. Milhard. He sounded his buzzer. "Sorry. You're inappropriately educated for the job."

He practically threw me out of the office.

Why did I feel so depressed as I walked to my car? I wouldn't touch Mr. Milhard and his rotten movies with a ten-foot pole; yet I had the feeling that *he* had rejected me. It must be all those power strategies he was using, the ones I'd scoffed at as too silly to bother learning. Everything he did seemed calculated to put you off guard. Even his unpronounceable name.

The hell with him, I thought: I've got my husband, my children, my charge-a-plate. I'll be all right, I'll be fine.

⚜ Chapter 33

When I got home from Creative Systems, Inc., I couldn't wait till dinnertime so I could tell Bert all about it. I went straight to the kitchen and whipped up a good meal. We'd have dinner and wine, and laugh about the preposterous Mr. Milhard. As I set the table, the phone rang.

"This is Dr. Hoffman's secretary at the Medical College," said an unfamiliar voice. "Dr. Hoffman asked me to call and let you know that he would be unable to be home for dinner."

"I see. Did he say why?"

"No, he didn't."

"Thank you."

I wanted to ask whether Dr. Hoffman had said when he would be home, but was too embarrassed.

I went back to the kitchen and considered stopping my soufflé in mid-bake, but it was already beginning to puff up. I gazed at the burgundy that I had opened and was letting breathe, at the salad glistening in the wooden bowl.

Donald came into the kitchen and stuck his head in the fridge. "Hi, Mom."

"Where's Barney?" I asked.

"He said to tell you he's eating with the band—"

"Well, I guess that leaves the two of us to eat this beautiful dinner I just cooked," I said.

"Not me! You were late so I made myself a couple of peanut butter sandwiches and finished off the angel-food cake."

"Oh."

"I'm gonna do my homework now, Mom," said Donald. "I fed and walked Fluffy and cleaned her box. I got a book report due tomorrow, so—"

"Do not disturb?"

"Right."

I sat at the dining room table alone. I poured myself a glass of wine, served myself some soufflé, and ate a few bites of salad. The room was deathly quiet. I could hear my fork scraping the plate. I wished I knew when Bert *would* be home. It was so unlike him to be vague or to delegate his call to a secretary. I kept thinking I heard Barney pulling in the driveway. I wanted to go to Donald's room and ask him when Barney had said he'd be home, but he had made it very clear that he needed to work, and I'd been preaching concentration all year.

I washed the dishes, re-corked the burgundy, and scraped the flat, disappointed-looking soufflé into the garbage. Some things can only be enjoyed when they're fresh: you wait for them as the recipe says—they don't wait for you.

Unable to concentrate on school work, I went into the study and turned on the TV: a pale man with asthma was coughing into the camera while a mournful announcer suggested a cough remedy—then several women with beautiful hair twirled their tresses around and assured us they were worth the best shampoo. One woman without a flaw on her face smoothed makeup over her skin and cooed, "Cover-All—for when you're over twenty-five."

Twenty-five, I thought—if that poor girl with her flawless skin, foot-long eyelashes, and silky hair was over the hill and going around scaring little children—what did that make me? I was thirty-eight—soon to be thirty-nine. And Bert was forty-eight—nearing the dangerous age.

I could barely grasp the plot of the show I watched; there were a lot of car crashes and burning buildings. At some point in the evening, Donald came in and switched the channel.

"I want to watch this one show before bed," he said.

"Did you finish your homework?" I asked.

"Yep."

More car crashes, more burning buildings.

"Oh, Mom," said Donald, during a commercial, "I forgot to tell you—Dad called."

"When?"

"When I got home from school. He said he was going to a department party. For somebody new."

"Why didn't you tell me?"

"I forgot."

"*Don*ald. I cooked that whole meal thinking he'd be here."

"Gee, I'm sorry, Mom," said Donald. "Can I get you something from the kitchen?"

He was out of the room before I could get my hands on him.

I fell asleep on the couch and had no idea when Bert got home.

The next evening, I cooked a good dinner again—if not quite so fancy as the one of the night before—and waited for Bert to arrive home.

"Missed you last night," I said. "Did you have a nice party?"

"It was more like a meeting," he said.

When had I heard an exchange like that before?

It dated back, if I wasn't mistaken, to the night I'd come home from Bob's party. But Bert was off to the bedroom to take off his tie and get comfortable before I could pursue the conversation. I had wondered at Bert's perfect tact that night; his "I trust you" had been so very sweet. I suspected that he was more suspicious and upset at my behavior than he had let on.

When he came back to the kitchen to make a drink, I said, "Donald told me you called to let me know you'd be gone for dinner—but he forgot to tell me till about eleven o'clock."

"I was afraid he might, so I asked Miss Kelly to call before I left for cocktails," said Bert. "I assumed you'd be late from your job interview and not feel like cooking much anyway."

"Yeah," I said.

"Cheers," said Bert. He gulped an ounce of martini. "Don't you want your drink?"

"Hmm? Oh, yeah." I took a little sip. I studied Bert. He looked great. Maybe it was the fact that Poppa was settled, and that my mother's wedding was postponed—or that spring was on the way.

"You used to hate department parties and meetings," I said.

"They're okay once in a while. The head of the department likes to get everybody together to meet new staff. Friedman is pretty interesting. We all had cocktails, dinner, a good discussion. You were asleep when I came in."

"I know."

"I should think you'd be all for my not hanging around here waiting to be waited on," said Bert.

"It's just—"

"I feel you've set a good example for me by getting out and doing more—enlarging your circle. Surely you want me to do the same—"

"Of course," I said.

"Isn't that one of the tenets of Women's Lib—that it means growth for men too?"

"Yes."

"You wouldn't want me to be the same old reliable, predictable Bert—"

He drifted off to the study.

Later that evening I joined him. He was reading *Open Marriage* and smoking a new pipe.

🔥 Chapter 34

My next job interviews didn't go much better than the one at Creative Systems, Inc. Dean Pointer sent me to a high school to investigate teaching a part-time course for which the students would get college credit. The school was forty-five minutes from my house and the salary only just covered the gasoline and mileage on the car. When I told the dean of my decision not to take the job, he looked cross—even when I explained my reasons.

"I thought being a married woman you wouldn't be so interested in salary."

I'd wondered why the entire faculty of the school I was sent to was female. When I told Bert of Pointer's reaction, he was furious.

"Ask him if he counts the women working at that high school in the percentage employed by City U. and the art department," he said.

"You're taking this harder than I am."

"My sacrifice has been great," he said. "Besides I'm going to lead a seminar on women in the professions; our residents need it."

"You only learned to make a sandwich last week."

Bert didn't hear me.

"Dr. Friedman thinks I'm uniquely qualified to lead

the group—partly because of your painless and quick re-entry into your field."

"Painless," I said.

I continued to seek interviews with prospective employers, but something always happened.

An art director at an advertising agency sounded very encouraging over the phone. He had asked for my grade transcripts and after reading them, had returned my call.

"Is this Laura Williams Hoffman?" he asked.

I said it was.

"I'd like to take you to lunch to talk about a job," he said.

"Fine."

"We pay quite well." He set our lunch date for the following noon.

When the man saw me, his jaw dropped. I don't know what he expected Laura Williams Hoffman to look like, but I obviously didn't fit the bill. Maybe my new frizzy hairdo was a bit too youthful. I had thought it looked pretty good with the slight tan I'd gotten at Quailridge Park.

"Your husband's a doctor?" asked the man.

"That's right."

"And where are you from?"

"Baltimore."

"You have a teeny bit of a Southern accent—a soft voice."

What was he getting at?

He watched me very closely as I ate, as though my food habits would give him some clue as to what made me tick.

"Did you like my sketches?" I asked.

"Oh—yeah," he said. "They're swell."

I was more uneasy every minute as he scrutinized my features.

"Is there anything wrong?" I asked.

"You *are* the wife of the Dr. Hoffman who's in the public health field, aren't you?"

"No, my husband teaches psychiatry at the General Hospital and takes private cases—"

The guy called for the check. He was very agitated. Maybe he was a former patient of Bert's. I hoped he wasn't violent.

"I'll call you," he said. We hadn't even had coffee or dessert. "Enjoyed talking to you."

He sure had cooled down.

"Who's the Dr. Hoffman in public health?" I asked Bert.

"Bill Hoffman. Black guy—prince of a fellow," said Bert.

I felt my kinky hairdo and looked in the mirror.

"Is Dr. Hoffman dark-skinned?" I asked.

"About a shade lighter than you. Why?"

"Ah specks ah done blew anutha interview."

The next man with a job opening told Mr. Newman he would like to interview me—once Mr. Newman told him I wasn't the other Mrs. Hoffman.

"I don't suppose you care to seek out a meeting," Mr. Newman said.

I couldn't cut it as a token black, and I wasn't willing to be the Great White Hope.

"I haven't sunk that low," I said. "Yet."

Kim came to the rescue.

"Laura, I've got a neat possibility for you. A friend of mine, Ivor Swan, runs the art department at Chic Clothes, and he needs an illustrator for ads. I told him you'd be perfect—you can do hands and feet and stuff and he said he'd be glad to see you—"

"Kim, *thanks*," I said. I jotted down the phone number she gave me.

"Remember one thing," she said, "so you don't put your foot in it. Ivor's a transvestite. If he acts peculiar, just ignore it. He's undergoing a crisis at the moment—wants to be a female—he's thinking of getting a sex change operation."

"Sounds logical."

"There's one problem. He's just not good-looking enough to be a woman. I mean, he'd never make it as a woman. I haven't seen him for a while; for all I know, he's done the thing. His voice sounded the same and I didn't question him because I don't want to be asked what I think of his new look."

What did I wear to this one? I wondered. I'd been reading the copy of *Dressing for Success* that Gail had given Barney for Christmas and had been wearing the conservative navy suit recommended for women who want to make it. But it seemed a little conventional for this interview. I put on my mid-calf peasant skirt; it was not bad-looking, but it called for four-inch heels—those torture implements I had sworn off in the fall.

Nevertheless, I felt "in," if foolish, when I reached the building where my interview with Ivor was to take place. Every other woman, with or without briefcase, and in spite of the fact that the April weather had turned rainy and cold, was wearing the same outfit: cotton skirt and open-toed sandals with pale stockings. We all looked as though we were freezing. I *was* freezing. The males wore sensible, warm shoes and dark suits.

All but Ivor. He was more colorfully attired in a two-tone raspberry shirt, a purple, Saville-Row cut suit, and Gucci loafers with no socks.

"You're Laura?" he asked. "Kim's told me all about you. Let's see your portfolio."

Ivor was clearly knowledgeable about art; he picked out the sketches that demonstrated the kind of drawing I'd have to do in his department.

"I want to show these to the higher-ups," he said.

Kim was right about Ivor's chances of becoming a desirable woman. He was quite homely; his body was decidedly masculine, with broad shoulders, long arms, and big hands.

"Your drawings are super," he said. "I think we can definitely use you—but of course I've got to check it out with my boss." He laid my résumé on his desk along with the drawings.

"I'll be calling you soon," he said. "I love your skirt."

"I guess I'd better be going."

"Oh, have a cup of coffee with me."

I accepted the coffee, and Ivor was soon telling me of his crisis.

"I'm a transvestite," he said.

I'd never had anyone confide this particular thing to me before. I tried not to look shocked; he announced it as though it were something like national origin.

"That's nice," I mumbled.

"I suppose Kim's told you. I'm going to get a change. What do you think?"

"I—"

"Be frank," said Ivor. "Kim says I'm too ugly, but I'm getting my shoulders broken and a nose job. I think that'll help." He looked in the mirror.

"You have a nice small waist," I said.

"Ah well—we shall see."

"Are these your sketches?" I asked, pointing to some drawings pinned on the wall.

"Indeed."

"They're good."

"Lucky at cards, unlucky in love."

"I really must go," I said. "I hope I hear from you."

"You will, you will," said Ivor. "And tell Kim to call me. She borrowed a dress from me and I need it back!"

I sincerely liked Ivor in spite of his strange way of introducing himself. I thought I would enjoy working with him and was anxious to sign up at Chic Clothes.

Three weeks went by and I didn't hear from Ivor. What could be wrong? He was so definite about liking my stuff. Feeling worse and worse, I finally approached Kim.

"He almost promised me the job and then I didn't hear from him," I said. "Does Ivor tend to tell you what you want to hear?"

"No—he's very straight when it comes to business," she said. "I'll call him and see what went wrong."

When I got to class at the next session, Kim was angry—at me.

"He hadn't read your résumé," she said. "You *didn't* put your *age* on it!"

"Of course I did," I replied.

"Well, he said the boss hit the ceiling when he recommended a near forty-year-old housewife with three children and a doctor husband. He said absolutely no and Ivor was too crushed to call you—he said you were so nice and you and he got along so well."

"What's wrong with being near forty?" I said. "I should be a good bet. I'm not going to get pregnant."

"Neither are most of the younger girls nowadays. Employers just won't sink the training and the insurance and health payments and the whole bit into anyone your age. The employee's an investment; they want twenty years of work."

"I can go twenty years—I'm in perfect health."

"But statistically, you're not. People in your age group are past their peak. And you're too affluent. You won't be easily intimidated."

"Neither will the young, and what am I to do? I can't help being thirty-eight."

"Let me see that résumé," she said.

I produced the incriminating document.

"Take off your birthdate and eliminate the husband and kids."

"What if they ask me about my age and marital status?"

"Lie," said Kim. "Now, Laura, will you write me a letter of recommendation for *my* résumé?"

Kim pulled out a document longer than Sister Margaret's.

"Just say what a good leader I was, how helpful, on the up and up morally, blah, blah, blah."

I wrote her a letter and gave it to her after class. She looked it over, frowning.

"You've signed it Laura Hoffman and it doesn't say who you are. You could be some dumb kid."

I was getting confused. She looked apologetic.

"For this, stress how mature you are, Laura, and sign it Mrs. Bertrand Hoffman, will ya? Thanks."

I could get an identity crisis, except that I was quickly learning that the world is full of people working up their résumés. I wrote the letter.

Everyone's résumé was getting fatter, except mine. When I deleted my age and my family, there was very little left. I put the date at the bottom of the page and gave it lots of white space. Maybe I should add Transportation Chairman, Boys' Choir, and Costume Design, "Children of Many Lands."

⚜ Chapter 35

As the final quarter progressed, we began to plan our student show, which was to open the day of graduation. In sculpture, I was trying to finish my many-armed figure that currently resembled an overweight octopus. In order to get the hard stone drilled away that would get her into more elegant proportions in time for the exhibit, I had to stay at the job steadily with my goggles and drill.

Mrs. Goldfarb worked at a string nest into which she would put the dozen suede eggs that she'd completed. Tony was doing a soft sculpture of a Battered Woman, and Mr. Rubel, having completed his magnum opus, was producing mysterious wax hands.

"Use 'em in my business," he said.

I shuddered whenever I saw him applying bright red fingernail polish to these ghoulish white members. Ron was very little help.

"I'm not into realistic modeling, Mr. Rubel. Too limiting," he said. "If you can dig it—go to it."

Mr. Rubel asked me for criticism and I gave it when I could.

"Fingers have a definite structure," I said. I sketched the bone system for Mr. Rubel. "They aren't like a bunch of bananas—you see?"

We arrived in painting class one morning to find Ms.

Saffron in a rage. She was sitting in her big wicker chair tapping her foot violently on the concrete floor.

"Something must be done," she said.

"What's up?" said Sister Margaret.

"Those bastard MCP's have kicked my uterus out of the faculty show."

I recalled the plastic womb she had suspended from the ceiling at her one-person exhibit.

"So I heard," said Sister, "but it's a space limitation—Mr. Newman said."

"And you *believe* him?"

"It's the size of the Hindenburg," said Sister Margaret. She had gotten very cocky since acquiring her job.

"Well—what about those twin phallic monstrosities that klutz Rubel made in Ron's class? They're making room for *them*."

"That does put a different light on the matter," said Sister.

"I'm going to demand a completely separate third show, for women only. Mrs. Goldfarb, you'll go along, won't you?"

Mrs. Goldfarb looked anguished.

"My husband's coming to graduation," she said. "I'd hate to spoil his day."

Ms. Saffron looked at her contemptuously.

"Dora?"

"Sure. Only I'm not sure we should exhibit at all. I wanted an extension on my paper, and Mr. Borges asked if I were having an extra period this month."

"Yeah," said Tony. "Maybe we should do more—demand the dean's resignation for only havin' one woman on the faculty or somethin'. I'm so tired of gettin' kicked around."

"That little shit Mr. James embarrassed me in front

of the whole class this week," said Sister. "I asked for a more private studio to do my independent study project in—he had me squeezed into a room with twenty people —and he said he guessed I needed a chastity screen."

Even Flo chimed in. "The male models always got to wear a jockstrap. We weren't even allowed a piece of drapery."

"I may bring suit," said Ms. Saffron.

Why not, I thought. Everybody on campus was suing everybody else. The black students were suing the political science department for racism. The Women's Caucus was suing Community Planning for sexism. The med school was being sued for reverse discrimination and the law school for having quotas. The government was suing the whole University for not complying with HEW rules. The campus police were in court for dope dealing, the president had been accused of violating a state contract, and the financial aid department was being investigated by the FBI.

"These are bad things to put up with," I said to the women, "but even worse, I think, is incompetence. I've been thinking of reporting Ron to the dean all year—but we can't throw everybody out at once—"

"Why not?" said Ms. Saffron. "The whole bunch ought to be put to sleep."

"Well—maybe you're right," I said. "I'm sick of Dean Pointer asking the men students how their work is going and me how are the children."

"He always asks me that, too," said Mrs. Goldfarb. "And I don't have any children."

I didn't say anything about Mr. Borges: after comparing notes with Sister, I'd found that he had never done anything worse than steal a kiss, and I didn't feel he was a real threat. I knew if I mentioned my experience to

Dora, Tony, or Ms. Saffron, they'd hustle me off to the Rape Crisis Center. And I was in no mood to be rehabilitated.

Ms. Saffron stood up.

"Write all these things you've said—and any others you can think of—and we'll print them on big posters. We'll have our own show. I'll tell Dean Pointer about it in the faculty meeting tomorrow. Are you all in? Mrs. Goldfarb?"

She was obviously equally terrified of Ms. Saffron and of Mr. Goldfarb.

"Let us know tomorrow before the meeting. Laura?"

"I don't know yet," I said. "I'll have to think about it. I'm concerned about using art for propaganda . . ."

"You have to bear witness," said Ms. Saffron.

"Yes, but I don't have to be fatuous," I said. "There's something a little trite about this—"

All the others, even Sister Margaret, glared at me.

I glared back. Oh, I was getting strong.

Or was I?

What I wanted to do was reserve judgment on this move of Ms. Saffron's until I could talk it over with Bert and Mr. Newman.

"Laura, you fink," said Sister. She had followed me down the hall after painting. "How come you aren't supporting Ms. Saffron's separate show? The faculty clearly used different standards for her sculpture and Mr. Rubel's —and you yourself were sent out to that cockamamie job in East Jesus—how much more do you need?"

"It's that I really don't like Ms. Saffron's work and her approach. Just making a lot of circles and vagina-shaped objects doesn't qualify junk as art. I have standards and I don't want to make an ass of myself. That won't gain respect for women."

"I see your point."

"You do?" I said. "You're a big help. I was hoping you'd twist my arm and make it easy for me."

Bert was all for my joining up with the women's group.

"We talked in the seminar last time about the need to publicize all forms of discrimination," said Bert. "The women in the group made quite a case. You exhibit with Mr. Rubel and others that aren't top flight in your opinion. Won't your stuff stand out if it's good—whether the others are good or not?"

"I don't know—surrounded by all that rhetoric—"

Mr. Newman took the opposite point of view.

"This is nonsense and you know it, Laura. Women's art, men's art. Who have you admired and understood as artists? Have they been of just one sex? There are only two kinds of artists: good and bad."

I nodded. He was so wise and reasonable.

"You're right," I repeated, "there are only two kinds of artists: good and bad."

I was halfway to the door of his office when I turned around.

"Except when you apply for a job," I said. "Then there are at least eight kinds—male and female, black and white, experienced and inexperienced, old and young."

I went to Ms. Saffron's office and joined up. I was going to be a little embarrassed by the twenty-five-foot uterus dominating our show, but what I felt good about was making up my own mind—especially when it didn't agree with Mr. Newman's.

⚜ Chapter 36

"Laura, would you mind fixing a light buffet and drinks for my seminar on Women's Lib? We meet here on Friday."

I started to point out the irony of Bert's request. The last thing I needed was to entertain. But I said okay. With this, I would work out the last of my guilt about Bob—which was still festering over that evening at his apartment. Besides, now I was worried about Bert—what with his more frequent evenings out and his reading matter. When he had finished *Open Marriage,* he had started *Beyond the Nuclear Family.* This was no time to quibble.

"We usually have drinks, beer, something like ham and roast beef, a few salads, pickles and olives—that kind of stuff—nothing too fancy," said Bert. "Some of the hostesses don't bother with dessert."

I scratched dessert off the list I was making.

"They just put out some brownies or something with the coffee."

It seems I was giving a dinner party on Friday.

"What time is this served?" I asked.

"About ten."

I'd be washing dishes and cleaning up until dawn. But

this would definitely clear the books as far as Bob was concerned. I promised myself that.

On Wednesday before Bert's meeting, I made a grocery list and tried to think about the buffet. I hadn't entertained since Christmas, and wasn't positive where the decent salt and pepper shakers were. Or trays. Or glasses. Or good forks.

I resolved to keep it simple—both the menu and the service. But entertaining informally is like going to social events "as you are." You have to buy a whole new outfit that looks as though you'd been wearing it and is still nice enough to appear in at a party.

The glasses and forks were covered with water spots from the dishwasher. In the spirit of my new life, I lined them up on the tray as is. Then the sun hit their leprous-looking surfaces; I held a glass up to the light. Disgusting. The whole batch had to be rewashed and dried. I didn't want Bert to be ashamed of his home. The other doctors' wives had probably done a beautiful job. Most of the ones in Bert's department were full-time homemakers.

Since Mother had cleaned the silver at Christmas, it hadn't been touched and was reverting to its old plum color.

Gritting my teeth at the time it took, and dodging leaflets for National Cottage Cheese Week and leftover newspaper coupons, I went through the supermarket. For this simple little snack, my list, actual and mental, went like this:

ham	
roast beef	
cheese	to fill out the meat platters—at the price of meat, buy the minimum
lettuce	to form a suitable bed for the meat and cheese

pickles		
olives		
mustard	don't forget to wash little dishes to	
mayonnaise	serve these in	
peppercorns	a must for Bert	
butter	in case there's a butter-freak in the crowd—I was going to skip it	
bread, rye, white	find the bread tray	
cocktail onions		
cocktail cherries	little dishes	
lemons	gotta slice them for the bar;	
limes	round up serving dish	
cocktail napkins	paper	Mother would never find out unless someone told her
dinner napkins	"	"
potato salad	in a carton	"
slaw	"	"
coffee	when did the price double?	
half-and-half	find the cream pitcher and don't forget to strain the lumps out of the sugar in the good sugar bowl	
candles		
mints	more little dishes to round up	
nuts		
brownies	unimaginative but could be eaten with the fingers	
tonic		
Coke	Bert could pick this up but he'd developed a cold and he was already	
club soda		
beer	Going to the Liquor Store for Me	

After battling the distractions of Muzak, premiums offered with every item, and the high finance of returning soda pop bottles, I came home with most of the items on my list, plus a hundred dollars worth of junk that had stowed away in my grocery cart.

Barney helped me put the stuff away.

"Can I throw out this leftover dip?" he said, trying to find space in the refrigerator.

"Has it gone bad yet?" I asked.

He pushed at it with his finger.

"You could use it for Tub Tite."

"Then pitch it," I said. "Would you eat these two bananas?"

He made a face.

"They look like the back of an old lady's hand."

"Will you stop with the colorful metaphors?" I said. "If I wanted to keep those bananas for something, they'd disappear in a minute."

Barney put them on the counter.

"Shouldn't be refrigerated anyway."

When we got all the stuff crammed into the refrigerator, the door wouldn't close.

"I should be thinking about how to light a painting," I said. "And be rounding up a pedestal for a lady with eight arms."

I put my weight against the door and tried to force it to stay closed. When I moved away it popped open.

"You'll have to eat the leftover chili, too," I said.

"Mom," said Barney, "you got another Lord Byron glass in the Famous Poets Peanut Butter series. We were up to Wordsworth."

Friday after school I worked at a hectic pace. Everything on my list of jobs was a last-minute item. Take the plastic covers (used because of the dog) off the dining room chairs, adjust the crooked lampshades, wipe the fingerprints off the doors, clean the downstairs bathroom. Go and pick up ice.

I slapped my forehead.

I'd forgotten a centerpiece.

The phone rang.

"Hi, Mom," said Gail.

"Gail!" I replied. "How are you?" I tried to dust the top of the sideboard as we talked. I was still thinking coffeemaker, electric cord, cups and saucers (they'd have to be wiped off after sitting unused in the pantry all those months).

"And so we've decided to get engaged," she said. "We'll probably have the ceremony sometime in August or September."

I wrote "Gail" in the dust on the sideboard.

"Mom?" said Gail. "Are you there?"

"Are you sure about this?" I said.

"Positive."

"I'll let you talk to your father."

I handed the telephone to Bert, who was just walking into the house.

"Your daughter," I said. "She's engaged."

Bert had a long chat with Gail while I tried to listen in and simultaneously deal with my own thoughts and feelings. I dusted the same piece of furniture over and over—taking both parts in the phone conversation. Bert pointed out the obvious—that Gail was very young for marriage, that she hadn't finished her education, that she'd only known Roy a year. Blah, blah. Which is just the way she obviously heard what her father was saying. He was not making even a small dent in her plans.

When Gail and Bert had finished talking, I got back on the phone. All I could offer were my best wishes and the promise that we'd talk when she got home. Bert said all there was to say at this point. When we hung up, I turned to him.

"Sounds pretty determined."

"We can't forbid it," said Bert.

"No—marriage is not against the law—maybe it should be, but it's not."

"Wow, you sound bitter."

"Well—she's too young to get married and Mother's too old—damn it!"

Bert looked afraid of me.

"I think I'll go to the liquor store," he said. "Is there anything I can get?"

"Ice," I said. "And I forgot the centerpiece."

When Bert returned I was trying to find room in the kitchen among the jars of olives, nuts, crackers, and dip for the family to eat the frozen dinners I was about to serve them.

"Do you want Mexican Fiesta or the Peking Platter?" I asked.

"Nothing for me," said Bert. "I'll just have a drink."

I snatched the glass from his hand.

"No! Don't mess everything up!"

"One drink—"

It seemed to me that the displacement of one ice cube would undo the whole carefully arranged kitchen.

"What's wrong, Laura?"

"All my plans are going wrong!" I said.

Bert shrugged.

"Anything I can do? Gee, you look white. I hope you aren't all worked up about this evening—it's supposed to be casual."

I ran into the hall to give the bathroom a last going-over. Barney and Donald had been forbidden to use this bath, but there was a towel floating in the tub, toothpaste all over the sink, and a cigarette butt in the toilet. I righted these wrongs and put linen guest towels in place of the grimy terrycloth.

When I checked the party trays, I noticed the edges of

the meat had turned up slightly; I had arranged things hours too early in a fit of frantic miscalculation.

At eight the doorbell rang. It sounded like a burglar alarm.

"I'll go," said Bert. He looked through the glass to the front porch. "Oh, it's Dr. Friedman."

I patted my messy hair and stood beside Bert to greet the members of the seminar.

"Come in," said Bert. "Melissa, I want you to meet my wife, Laura. Laura, Dr. Friedman."

Bert's colleague and co-leader in the seminar was about five feet seven and weighed no more than 108 pounds. Her long blond hair hung glamorously over her shoulders and her hazel eyes were bright with intelligence. She was about twenty-eight years old, and worth the more expensive shampoo.

The others in the group were younger than I had imagined, too: a few men students, but mostly women psychiatric residents and fledgling doctors. When everyone was assembled, we sat around in a circle in the living room and Bert opened the seminar. The discussion dealt with the same kind of attitudes and frictions that I'd encountered at school and in job-hunting. There were echoes of Kim and assertiveness training. The group very politely included me in the conversation and I got lots of praise for adapting to my new role and for joining the women's art show.

But Bert was the star of the evening. He was so up on the problems of the working mother, so tuned in to the needs of women, so in favor of family flexibility. Bert— who as of last month would have gone to war over whether a pot roast should be basted.

As "Melissa" put it as she munched daintily on a sandwich: "Bert's the only man on the senior faculty who understands the dissatisfaction we feminists feel with the profession."

After the meeting, everyone shook my hand at the door and thanked me for a lovely supper. With all these young people and working women in the group, the elaborate spreads that Bert had described, and that I had glamorized in my mind, must surely have come from Sam's sandwich shop.

But where did the Dr. Melissa Friedmans come from? From the same toy factory that turned out Kim? The world seemed to be taken over by fragile-looking young women in gauzy blouses who aren't afraid of anyone or anything.

I finally finished up the dishes and put away all the stuff I'd dragged out of the pantry. I sat down with a drink of my own.

Bert, looking ten years younger than when he'd gotten home from work, came into the kitchen and said, "Well, that went off with a minimum of fuss, didn't it?"

I didn't answer.

"What did you think of Melissa Friedman?" he asked.

"She's darling."

"She's one of the brightest residents we've ever had. Creative. Ambitious. She reminds me of Ethel Schmerz."

In the next few weeks I got thoroughly tired of hearing Melissa's name on Bert's lips. I had never thought of Bert as the sort of man who would be vamped by a younger woman. But then, he'd probably never pictured me smoking marijuana or passed out in some young man's bed. I began to worry when Bert worked late or had to go to evening "meetings," "parties," "seminars," or "conferences."

♨ Chapter 37

When I met my mother at the airport in May I was wearing blue jeans and long white gloves. As Barney had gotten more conservative and conventional in his dress, I began to look more like the Phantom of the Opera. The stone dust raised by my carving had irritated my fungus and both arms were covered with a scabrous rash. The white gloves, which were to prevent further infection, occasionally became yellow as the rash oozed; the greenish medicine I used also stained the fabric and didn't help the general impression.

"Laura," said Mother, "you look awful!"

"I know," I said, "I'm sorry. There's a rash on my arms. A combination of dust, fungus, and stress. So says your future husband."

"The gloves don't go with the blue jeans."

"Gloves with pus oozing through them don't go with anything," I said. "You don't want me to try matching them up with a silk print, do you?"

"A fine welcome," she sniffed.

"I'm sorry," I said.

She glanced at my arms on the ride home.

"I hope that clears up by the wedding."

"It can't be too soon for me. Really."

"Barney looks wonderful!" said Mother, after we'd had our first family dinner. "He looks quite handsome now that he's given up that ludicrous costume."

"The haircut helps too," said Bert. "He doesn't look like Tiny Tim anymore."

"John Travolta is more like it."

"I'll never know what happened to change Barney so quickly," said Bert. "Of course, I've always put my faith in letting kids work things out without too much interference—"

"I just hope he doesn't go too far," I said. "He's practically carrying a briefcase and he's being rushed for a fraternity. He does sort of do things all or nothing at all."

Mother had accepted my modification of her wedding plans without too much resentment. She was happy, looking younger than ever, and she wrote all the invitations to the wedding herself.

"You don't mind if I scrub and wax the stairway, do you, Laura?" she asked. "I don't want to rush you, but I can be getting a few things done ahead."

"Fine," I said. "Just let me get this show and graduation over with, and I'll give you my full attention."

"I don't suppose you'd have time to go to a shower on Saturday, would you?"

I didn't, but I said of course I would. What daughter would want to miss her own mother's wedding shower?

I received a slight shock before we left the house: the sight of Bert adjusting his tie in front of the hall mirror. He was dressed in a new sports coat and snappy gray slacks and loafers. He usually worked in the garden or in his workshop on Saturdays.

"Going out?" I asked.

"I'm having lunch with Melissa," he said.

"Oh."

I could hardly object. Did I want Bert objecting the day I'd had lunch with Bob—or any other day? A relationship between colleagues could be perfectly platonic—enriching.

Still, I felt less than perky as Mother, Aunt Edith, and I drove down Egmont Place, a tree-bordered private lane in the most exclusive section of Cincinnati. It was a cool, sunny day in late May. Perfect for a bridal shower, or anything else. I was determined to be pleasant. It was Mother's big day.

"So this is what the great world outside a painting studio looks like," I said.

We pulled into our hostess's driveway. Everything was perfect: every blade of grass was crisp and green, myrtle bloomed under the star magnolias and banks of daffodils and narcissus filled the slopes around the house. The house was perfect too: there were no dog's claw-marks on this door.

I checked my gloves. So far they were white and looked only mildly insane with the old navy silk sheath I had resurrected for the occasion. My arms were itching like fire. I rubbed one gently against my side. I'd like to use sandpaper, a nail file, my electric drill.

The door opened and Mother and the hostess, her best friend, were in each other's arms.

"Hortense!"

"Gladys!"

When they had done kissing and exchanging compliments, Mother said, "You know my daughter Laura and her sister-in-law, Edith Hoffman. Laura has this terrible rash. She's finishing her degree, you know."

Hortense looked at my arms with suspicion.

"Of course. Come in."

As we filed into the perfect hall—white woodwork, central staircase, antique game table, bowl of fresh flowers—Mother adjusted the edge of my right glove and patted it into place. Looking around the room, I decided I wasn't too crazily dressed, except for the gloves. All the other women—mostly Mother's age, but some mine, were wearing silk sheaths, dress-and-jacket combinations, or old Lillys. They all had dry skin.

Hortense had put up card tables in the living room, each with its own little pink or yellow cloth and bowl of daisies. A black woman in a white uniform kept peeking through the louvered kitchen door to see if it was time to serve the buffet.

As we stood awkwardly about, Hortense's daughter, a woman a few years older than I, brought around glasses of a sparkling beverage.

Thank God, I thought, champagne. I needed something to take my mind off the itching. I poured the cold liquid down my throat.

"Um," I muttered. I turned away from the group I was talking to. I will not throw up, I thought.

"It's sparkling grape juice—isn't it yummy?" I heard Hortense saying above the rising voices.

"Delish." "Where do you get it?" "So refreshing."

I looked around to see if anyone else was gagging on the sweet drink, but they all looked happy. What I wouldn't have given for a gin and tonic.

The door opened and closed, and more women, all dressed in blinding pinks and yellows and kelly greens, arrived at the party. The noise level moved toward a shriek.

Everyone was trading recipes and discussing the new fabrics or talking about their kids. I had forgotten this world existed.

At lunch—pastel green Jell-O, chicken à la king, and brownies—I found myself seated with Aunt Edith, Hortense's daughter Maude, and four other women.

"Well," said Maude, "now that you're about to get your degree, are you ready to be Laura Hoffman, housewife, again?"

A blob of green Jell-O fell from my fork.

"I'm afraid not," I said, as gracefully as I could. "I'm trying to get a job where I can use my training."

All eyes turned toward me.

"What about Donald?" said Maude. "Doesn't he need care?"

"Sure," I said. "But he's going to day camp this summer and then he'll be back in school."

"He must do well at school," she murmured.

"Great," I lied. "He won the spelling bee this spring." What on earth was wrong with me? I looked down at my arms. Faint yellow and green spots were beginning to appear on my gloves. I looked over at my mother, happily ensconced next to the hostess.

She looked younger than I did. She was having a romance: but then wasn't everyone except me? Gail and Roy were engaged and Poppa was still working on Mrs. Ratterman. Bert was having "lunch" with Melissa. I was putting quotation marks around everything in "life," a sure sign of mental derangement: I was a failure all the way around.

Mother laughed gaily at something Hortense said. She blushed. She was enjoying herself, I thought. Betrayed. I didn't know her. I'd always thought of Mother as somewhat sour—a compulsive cleaner, a frustrated wife. Now she was looking like a movie star and marrying someone who was not my daddy.

How childish can you get? I asked myself. I like Herbert. I must straighten out my act.

If I were happier about my own situation I wouldn't

have these puerile thoughts. Mr. Milhard, Ivor, "Dr." Friedman, and Dean Pointer paraded through my mind, ganging up on me with these women.

"Have some more chicken à la king," said Hortense. She had appeared at our table bearing a bowl of beige goo.

"It's my own special recipe. I put sherry in it."

"Yes, thank you," I said. She refilled my plate. I tried to strain the sherry out with my teeth and swallow it separately, but it was no go.

Our table was back on children again and each woman gave a rundown of what Gary, Cheryl, Peter, Benjamin, and Jennifer, or what have you, were up to. Most of the "children" were in their late twenties and thirties. The summaries sounded rehearsed.

"Gary is in China with the State Department, Peter is still at Brown—he's going to graduate magna cum laude. Benjamin is in Tokyo learning more Japanese. He's translating the ancient scrolls of Unomono. Jennifer is having her third baby as soon as she finishes her residence in brain surgery."

I didn't believe a word of it. And I'd felt crummy for one little lie about a spelling bee.

"How about yours, Maude? What's Boris up to?"

"He's starting a new business in Massachusetts," said Maude.

If I knew Boris, it was on a street corner in Cambridge near the subway, and it wasn't legal. Boris was thirty-five and the last time I'd seen him, his life's work was getting his head together and being "pretty deep into macramé."

The woman next to me was listing her children's accomplishments now: "Susie has one more year at Smith and then she takes a job in Rome. Roger is putting together his one-man show at the Guggenheim. Tracey gets her Ph.D. in June and they've offered her tenure and a staff of fifteen if she'll stay on and teach."

When they asked me about my family I blurted out, "Barney gets out of the pen next week, Gail has a job selling storm windows over the phone, and Donald—well, the teacher wants him to go on tour with the spelling bee."

Maude smacked me on the wrist.

"Oh, Laura," she said, "you're such a *character*."

Where she touched my hand, a large greenish-yellow spot appeared on my white glove.

I felt alone. I was no longer one of these women. I didn't know a single recipe and didn't have even a new Lilly. Why had I drawn attention to myself? Now the group was back "on my case," as Barney would say.

"Laura always had a great sense of humor," said one of the women.

"You'll do well in the arts."

"I just don't see how you *manage* with the children and all. Of course, I always say *something's* got to give."

She glanced at my arms. I was not just a character, I was a ghoul, turning rotten.

"I took some courses in literature once," said Maude, "but it interfered so with the family. Who does the ironing, Laura?"

I thought of the ironing: I had put it in the freezer—just for a while to keep it from mildewing—some months ago. It was no doubt frozen solid.

Support came from an unexpected source. Edith said, "I think Laura's very right to go back to her career now. It may be difficult, for a while, but if you wait too long, you never do anything at all."

Dead silence.

"I wanted to be a writer once."

My jaw fell open. I scratched my arm.

"Oh, yes," said Edith. "Long before Bert ever met you. But I felt Poppa needed me after Mama died—and then I waited till the canning season was over, and then the Christmas holidays, and then—"

"Oh, *Edith,*" I said, "I never dreamed—"

"Oh, I was quite the toast of Greenwich Village—"

"You lived in Greenwich Village?" I said.

On the way home, I thought, I've just got to get a job, I've got to get a job—I could be sucked back into the basement like a moth into a vacuum sweeper. I'd be condemned to a life of Hortense's luncheons—or I'd end up like Judy and the Cuisinart crowd. Or Edith.

I was talking to myself as Mother and I pulled into the driveway at home. I went straight to my room and pulled off my soaking, putrid gloves. Bert was home, and he looked amazed as I dumped my navy dress and pumps into a Goodwill bag. I would have slammed out of the house like Nora, but both the front and back door were stuck because of the painters. I could go through the porch, but it wouldn't be the same with sliding doors.

"What's the matter?" asked Bert. He sat on the bed beside me while I shivered with my head under the covers. "You seem upset."

That Bert. All those years of reading little gestures hadn't gone to waste.

I told him about my day.

"Something will turn up," he said.

"That's what Chamberlain said, and Hoover, and Johnson."

"But, Laura—"

"I've just about killed myself with work and probably wrecked my marriage going back to school—for what? So I can give luncheons like Hortense? Why did I think there were lines of employers waiting to seduce me into something nasty like commercial art? I can't even get a job doing ads—"

"What do you mean you've wrecked your marriage?" said Bert.

"Bert, you had 'lunch' with Melissa Friedman and you talk about her all the time. You've bought a whole new wardrobe since she joined the department and you've been looking like Gregory Peck in that picture with Tuesday Weld! I'm going out of my mind!"

"You're kidding," Bert said in a high, squeaky voice. "You think there's something between me and Melissa? I've got three kids!"

"And a wife," I said.

"And a wife," he added. "I'm on your team, Laura."

I burst into tears.

"There, there," Bert said, patting my shoulder. "I've merely been trying to learn from Melissa. You took me off-guard with all these sudden changes. You know my family is not the most avant-garde group in the world—"

"I've taken myself by surprise too," I said. "I've been like a snake—shedding skins and skins and skins."

"You've also shed ten pounds and about fifteen years," said Bert. "You look great—and I like you even better than before. I hate to say this, Laura, but before you went back to school you were becoming just a little bit—well —dull."

"As a plaster saint," I muttered, "or a model mom."

"So you haven't wrecked your marriage if that's any consolation."

"Well, of course it's a consolation." I put my arms around his neck.

"I thought I'd been very cooperative ever since you said you were going back to school. Haven't I been?"

"Well, yes," I said, "but I'm still ironing your shirts and sheets because you hate polyester. Except for keeping the books, I still do everything in the house."

He grinned sheepishly.

"You can throw me out anytime you want."

"What do you mean?"

"I put the house in your name," he said. He looked out the window to avoid what Kim called "eye contact"—like a little boy who has brought his sweetheart a rose.

"I'm going to do the same with half our assets, or whatever you think fair," he said. "I thought over what you've been saying."

For once I was speechless.

"I don't suppose this changes your mind about a job," said Bert.

"Not really," I said. "Just about you."

"When the wedding's over, we're going to go on a honeymoon," said Bert, "just the two of us."

"Bert—that's the most romantic thing I've ever heard."

"Really? Taking a trip?" he asked.

"No—putting some of our assets in my name."

He gave me a kiss and stood up.

"I'm going to make you a nice daiquiri after dinner," he said.

"I'll be there."

Bert walked over to the dresser and straightened his tie in the mirror.

"Which picture was it?" he asked.

"What do you mean?"

"With Gregory Peck and Tuesday Weld?"

"The one where he was the sheriff and she had an incestuous father—" I suddenly realized he was needling me, and maybe had been for a while. "Oh, what's the difference?"

"I don't see how you dreamed up that stuff about Melissa Friedman; what would a young girl like her see in a stuffy old guy like me?"

"I'll tell you later," I said.

* * *

When Mr. Rubel called that night to offer me a job, I took it.

Making wax hands and feet in a mortuary was not exactly what I had in mind as a career when I decided to go back to school, but at least it was honest work.

Chapter 38

"Gross," said Barney when I announced my job to the family.

"Of course, it's only part-time," I said, "but it pays pretty well."

The children looked crestfallen when I revealed my salary.

"Howie's mom is a stockbroker and makes twenty-five thousand a year," said Donald.

"The important part," said Bert, "is that you'll still have time for some original stuff of your own. That's what you really enjoy."

"And this way we can go to England."

"After you've worked for five years," said Barney.

"Or we could start financing some improvements on the cottage," said Bert.

"Oh no you don't, not with my money."

"Our money," said Bert. "Remember?"

As we were undressing for bed, Bert said, "I think I'll give a luncheon."

Like Barney he was slow to change, but once a trend hit him he went with it all the way.

"A luncheon?" I said. He was the very model of the model Liberated Husband.

"Yes, on the day of your show and graduation. It'll be a little pre-wedding celebration too, when Gail and Roy get here and the kids are around and before Herb and your mother take off. Who should I invite of your friends?"

I gave Bert a guest list and went on undressing. As I started to remove my gloves, Bert said, "Now that your immediate future is more settled and some of your conflicts are solved, that ought to be greatly improved."

I pulled back a white cotton glove. My arm looked like Gorgonzola cheese.

"It'll be better tomorrow," he said.

As the family reassembled, life was like a repeat of Christmas. Once again Mother and I went to the airport to meet Gail and Roy.

The two prospective brides embraced with girlish camaraderie. They compared engagement rings. Gail was wearing a large diamond, but her ambitions seemed to have shrunk. She was planning to spend the summer typing Roy's articles for the *Law Review*.

At dinner there was much joking about the upcoming weddings.

"Don't flash that rock around too much, Sis," said Barney. "It's a wonder you didn't blind the pilot and cause a plane crash."

Mother refused to tell where she and Herbert were going for their honeymoon, but Roy had definite ideas about his and Gail's.

"I've always wanted to go back to Bermuda, so we're going there," he said. "We thought about East Hampton but there are too many women in pantsuits with matching jackets and slacks."

"Horrible," said Bert.

* * *

When dinner was over, I went to bed early, and pretty soon came a knock at the door.

"May I come in and talk?"

It was Mother.

She sat on the edge of my bed and drew her feet up under her. In her white lace nightgown and robe and with her face scrubbed clean of makeup, she looked even younger than she usually did.

"I hope you're—well—happy I'm getting married again, Laura."

"Of course," said I.

"I sometimes feel—maybe you don't quite approve."

"It's hardly my business."

"That's true," said Mother, "it's not. On the other hand—I don't want you to feel that I've somehow—betrayed you—"

I swallowed hard.

"It's just—well, it's hard to think of you as anything but My Mother. I have to get used to you in your new role. I keep thinking what Daddy missed—"

"We were too young for marriage," she said.

"I really like Herbert."

Mother's eyes shone.

"He is a wonderful man—"

I hoped she'd spare me any intimacies: a little gushing over your mother's future husband goes a long way.

"He's the most wonderful bridge partner I've ever had," she said.

Relieved, I gave her my blessing and kissed her good night.

After she left, I returned to my book, a family saga set in the Yukon.

Another knock at the door. This time it was Gail, also

dressed in a virginal nightie. She jumped into bed beside me.

"I hope you're happy about me and Roy getting engaged," she said.

"I'm for whatever will make you happy."

"I was afraid you didn't like Roy. You don't seem ecstatic over our announcement."

"It's just that you're so young, Gail," I said. "I got married awfully young and I've always wished I'd grown up a little first. I always felt torn about not developing my painting."

"If I want a career later, I'll just go get it—like you did."

I sighed.

Gail looked at my reading matter.

"Is that a good book?"

"The first three thousand pages were enthralling," I said. "The second half drags a little." I put it down.

"Mom," said Gail, "doesn't it seem—strange—my grandmother and I both engaged at the same time?"

"It is a little unusual."

"When I was a child I used to think of grandmothers as little old ladies with gray hair and canes."

"I thought of mothers the same way."

"Do you think Grandmaw is marrying Herbert for sex?"

I had just been wondering the same thing.

"Not that alone, I'm sure," I said. "They share a lot of interests—but your grandmother's about—let's see—fifty-nine—and he's in his mid-sixties. It's not outside the realm of possibility."

"Yuck," said Gail. "Obscene at their age."

She looked at me with appraising eyes.

"Doesn't it ever stop? The sex urge?" she said.

"Well, look at Poppa chasing Mrs. Ratterman," I said, "and one of the men in the nursing home just shot his sweetheart out of jealousy—"

"You're kidding."

"It was in last week's paper. He's eighty-eight."

"That's absurd," said Gail. "I mean, I'm all for it when you're young—but there *are* other things in life."

"Name one."

She looked at me with surprise.

"How about your painting—your artwork?"

"I was exaggerating, of course. But as I get closer to forty, my concept of when people stop being interested in sex extends to a later and later age—if ever."

Gail looked puzzled, as though she were seeing me for the first time.

"Well," said she briskly. She examined the cover of my book again. " 'Four generations of tumultuous passion, unconquerable pride, tormented destinies, all set against the background of the harsh, unconquerable tundra of the Yukon.' Do you want some cocoa, Mom?"

"Are you making?"

"Yes," said Gail. "By the way," she added, not moving, "I have a confession to make that I think is going to shock you pretty badly."

Oh, oh, thought I. An abortion? She's pregnant? What?

"Roy and I want a traditional wedding."

I could feel my hair relax.

"Is that all? It's okay by me."

"Well—it's not going to help your career along to be planning another big wedding—but Roy and I will do all the work. I know it sounds—regressive—after I helped push you into school and everything. But Roy and I want a real home and a family like you and Daddy have."

"That's wonderful, Gail. But you mustn't romanticize. No marriage is perfect."

"I know, but you've been married longer than anyone I've ever heard of."

"Twenty years?"

"That's right. When I was a little girl I used to wish sometimes you and Daddy would get a divorce so I could be more chic, like my friends!"

"Oh, Gail—you still seem like a little girl to me."

"Actually, I'm quite realistic and grown-up," she said. "I'm not completely starry-eyed. I know Roy's a little bit stuffy, but he's really so sweet."

"If you care for him, he's got to have something . . ."

"I figured Daddy's a little stuffy—and look how well he turned out." She left me to my family saga.

☗ Chapter 39

Bert's luncheon was beautiful.

"I'm going to do this more often," he said as he presided at the carefully set table. "In the group I'm leading on new patterns and sex roles, we've been talking about the fact that most men never take on any of the social chores of a family. Thus they deprive themselves of a lot of pleasures that women enjoy—"

"That's true, Daddy," said Gail.

"Down, girl," said Roy. "No Women's Lib in my home."

Gail did not say a word. She just beamed.

"I'm talking about Men's Liberation," said Bert. "I had immense fun doing this luncheon—"

"But you didn't do it exactly the way a woman would have," said Kim.

"Right," said Sister Margaret.

Bert had gotten his secretary to call the guests and he'd hired a cateress with two helpers to set the table, cook, and serve the food. He poured the wine.

I thought of all the hours I'd spent on similar occasions grinding tiny bits of leftover ham into ham salad and trying to find the cheapest cherry tomatoes in town. But I was in no mood to complain. With my family, friends, and future employer gathered around, I felt so good my arms didn't itch.

"Excellent wine, Mr. Hoffman," said Roy.

"Glad you like it, Roy," said Bert, "and now a toast to the graduate and the June bride."

Mother and I both beamed.

"The last time I tried to drink a toast here, I had to deliver puppies," said Herbert.

"Fluffy's spayed," said Donald. "That means she had a hysterectomy."

"Herb knows that, Donald," said Bert.

Mr. Rubel raised his glass and said, "To my new waxman."

"Wax-person," shouted half-a-dozen voices.

"Gross," whispered Barney.

"Wait," said Mr. Rubel, "I have something I want to announce."

We gave him the floor.

"Laura, I told the minister at the Episcopal church about you and he wants to talk to you about designing a stained-glass window in honor of a patron who just died."

"He *does?*" I said. "Me?"

"He has a fund to finance it and can pay about two thousand dollars."

"My God, I'd do something like that *free,*" I said.

Kim clutched her forehead. Bert made that rattling noise in his throat.

"I mean—could he raise a few more dollars?" I asked.

"He might," said Mr. Rubel, without noticing Kim and Bert. "That congregation is loaded with money. Only first-class funerals from there. Always."

"The thing is," said Sister, "if you get one commission like that it might lead to others."

I w⌐s thinking maybe I'd leave the gloves home when we left for commencement.

*　　*　　*

While we were having dessert, my father called and Judy, who had refused our lunch invitation, dropped in almost simultaneously.

"Thank you for the flowers," I said into the phone. "They're beautiful."

"Will you be staying home now, Laura?" said Daddy.

"No, I have a job," I said. "I'm—I'm doing a stained-glass window for a church."

"That's nice."

He asked to speak to the others, and Donald, Barney, and Gail took turns saying hello.

"I'm playing on a baseball team," said Donald. "We had a big game last week and we beat College Hill Cleaners. Guess what their team wrote on the wall of the boys' restroom?"

I heard incoherent grumbling as Donald held the receiver away from his ear.

"They wrote 'College Hill can beat Cincinnati Camera'!"

While Barney and Gail took their turns with my father, we greeted Judy. She was dressed in tennis clothes.

"What's new?" I said.

"You heard Terry split?"

"No!"

"Took the yogurt culture with him and went to the West Coast," she said. "The bastard."

We offered her some dessert.

"No, thanks."

She had lost another ten pounds and looked like a twenty-five-year-old.

"I'm on a strict diet and I leave for the fat farm next week."

"But, Judy," we all said at once, "you're so slim." "You don't need it," etc.

"I want to get down to size six," she said.

Her complexion looked wonderful too.

"Elizabeth Arden," she confided. "I take a whole day every time I go to New York."

We tried to persuade her to go to the graduation ceremony, but she refused. She picked up her racket.

"My backhand needs work. I play singles every Monday, Wednesday, and Friday, and doubles on the other days."

She gave me a peck on the cheek.

"You ought to try tennis, Laura," she said. "It's so good for you."

She sounded like a born-again Baptist.

"I've given up smoking since I started tennis, and I jog instead of cocktails."

"How's Millicent?" I asked.

"Recuperating. She just had all her body hair removed by electrolysis. She's going to look great."

She tucked her white sweater around her infinitesimal waist, waved good-bye, and left.

"Boy, does Judy look smart," said Mother.

"She really into vanity," said Barney.

Luckily, I don't need all that, I told myself. I have a family, a job, a degree.

"Gotta go get my graduation robe," I said. I rushed upstairs to the bedroom. I checked my backside in the mirror. When I took hold of a handful of flesh and pushed upward, it didn't look half bad.

The student gallery at School was a riot of plastic, rubber, rusty metal, and old shoes. Someone had shellacked a dead bird and an ancient Monopoly set. The paintings Flo had posed for were cubes, lines, squiggles, embossed white circles.

Flo greeted us absentmindedly. She was studying a sheet of Plexiglas with a neon tube connected to it; it was entitled "Flo." Her Rubensesque cheeks blushed pinker.

"I could just *die*," she said.

Donald was staring at Mr. Rubel's twin monsters that just cleared the ceiling.

"What on earth are those, Mom?"

"I'm going to ask Mr. Rubel what they are," I said. "I've wondered all year."

Barney leaned his head back to see the tops.

"Big mothers," he muttered.

The boys and I moved on to the women's show where Ms. Saffron's blimp all but blocked the light from the other work. Ms. Saffron had Roy and Gail backed into a corner.

"Freud says—" I heard Roy say.

"Freud sucks!" shouted Ms. Saffron.

Barney looked on, bemused.

"The Incredible Hulk meets Godzilla," he whispered.

Bert came up to me and said, "God, I pity that poor bastard Roy—has he got a way to go—"

"Here's Mom's stuff!" yelled Donald.

"Neat," said Barney.

They walked around the woman with eight arms.

Bert studied the sculpture very carefully and critically.

"You know, Laura," he said, "you're really quite good."

I sighed deeply.

"Well, I knew that," he said. "But your stuff really looks ten times better up here in the light of day than in the basement."

"Maybe I won't always be a wax-person," I said.

"I'm sure not," he said. "Incidentally, are you trying to say something by giving your woman eight arms? I feel it's symbolic somehow."

Barney was studying my painting.

"I may take some art courses myself this summer," he said.

"Really?" I asked. I was pleased though surprised. "I thought you were going to Kentucky Lake with the Phi Delts."

"I'm thinking of not pledging after all," Barney said. "I'm not really into beer and vomiting."

In the faculty gallery I introduced Bert to Mr. Newman and Ron. I told Mr. Newman about my church commission and he smiled like a proud father.

"You're a Virgo, aren't you?" Ron asked Bert. "I can see it in the aura shining around your head."

As we moved on to greet Mr. Sanders, Bert said, "Your friend Ron is not okay."

"*Are* you a Virgo?" I asked.

"As a matter of fact I am, but that has nothing to do with Ron's mental health."

Mr. Sanders gave us both respectful handshakes. To me he said: "Your work shows definite awareness of the dual nature of man—of art and life, of good and evil. Zeitgeist in the thoroughly heuristic meaning of the word."

"What on earth was he talking about?" whispered Bert as we moved away.

"He means on the great Quest-Journey of Life, I have purchased a Trip-Tick—I don't know . . ."

Mr. Borges came up to us, looking sour. He was wearing a Band-Aid on his head which I tried to avoid looking at.

"Your friend Harper's back," he said.

"Bob?"

I blushed from head to toe.

"Right over there."

There was nothing to do but go and greet him.

"Why aren't you in Pakistan?" I said.

"Starting back to school this summer," said Bob. "The Peace Corps 'deselected' me."

"Oh, I'm sorry."

"I'm not," said he. "I wasn't right for it. I like your stuff, Laura—"

"Hi, Bob," said Bert. He looked around the gallery. "Am I going to meet Crawley?" he asked.

"I don't think so," said Bob. "The state caught up with him."

"Good afternoon, Mrs. Hoffman," said Dean Pointer, "and how are the children?"

"They have diarrhea," I said.

I stared him right in the eye.

"Wonderful—give them my best." He and a companion moved off among the dignitaries.

Bob was doubled over with laughter.

"Do you know who that was with him?" asked Bert, also laughing and slapping Bob on the back. "The president of the University."

A student marshal announced that the graduating seniors should report to the Field House to dress for the procession. Before I left, Bert whispered, "You're right, Laura. Bob'd be perfect for Gail. Maybe we could invite him to your mother's wedding."

"It's too late," I said. "You can't fight true love."

"How could Gail love anyone that stuffy?" he asked.

While we seniors dressed in our black robes and mortarboards, we shouted obscenities at the administration for making us rent such hot, expensive outfits.

"It's a hundred and twelve in the shade out there!" said Dora. "And we're sitting in the sun."

"The brass gets the shady section!"

"And all we get to keep of these eighteen-buck outfits is the tassel on the hat!" said Sister. "Don't they know some of us are poor?"

"I don't mind," said Mrs. Goldfarb. She smiled for the first time since I'd known her. "My husband is proud of me. At last."

We did look impressive as we marched, all dressed alike, into the football stadium. I could tell because there were lines and lines and lines of identical figures before and after us. We crossed the football field and filled the seats like a long line of black ants: 15,000 people, mostly unemployed.

We fanned ourselves with our program as the president of City U. introduced the trustees, the recipients of honorary degrees, the deans of the colleges.

"Wish I'd worn pale blue or something—I'm sure my family doesn't know which one is me," I said to Sister Margaret.

Some of the students were dozing and others shredded their programs into confetti to throw when their class was announced. We slowly fried in the heat as the speaker assured us that "commencement" meant a beginning and not an end in our young lives.

"I know what Mr. Rubel's sculptures are for," I whispered to Sister.

"Bookends for large-print books?" she asked.

"No—he's going to put one on each side of the driveway at the funeral home."

"How banal," she said. "Oh, oh, there's our music."

"And now," said the president, "it is my pleasure to grant the degree of Bachelor of Arts to the members of the graduating classes of the colleges of Liberal Arts and the

School of Art and Design. Will the members of these colleges please rise to signify the granting of their diplomas?"

We stood. Our diplomas would arrive in the mail. And to think I'd dreamed of walking up all alone to the podium and having the president shake my hand.

"Is this it?" I asked.

The audience and our fellow students clapped and cheered and some of the nearby graduates threw their homemade confetti into the air.

"Is this all we get?" said Sister. "After all that work?"

"This and a tassel," I said.

The minute of applause died down and a piercing yell rang out across the stadium. I'd know Donald's voice anywhere: "Way to go, Mom!"